# Historical Footnotes
# of Santa Clara Valley

# Historical Footnotes

## *of Santa Clara Valley*

by Jack Douglas
San Jose Historical Museum Association
1993

Design and graphics by
Digital Typography & Design
2925 Varden Avenue
San Jose, CA 95124-1673

Printed in  USA by
The Rosicrucian Press
76 Notre Dame Avenue
San Jose, CA 95113

Editor: Kathleen Muller
Cover photograph courtesy of Pat Hathaway.
Published by San Jose Historical Museum Association.
Limited first edition, 1993.

ISBN 0-914139-10-X

*For my wife Kathryn*

# Contents

Introduction     viii
Acknowledgments     ix
Andrew Jackson Grayson—The Audubon Of The West     1
The Loves and Trials of Brigadier General Henry M. Naglee     5
Sarah Knox-Goodrich     11
Mary Hayes-Chynoweth     13
Our Phelan Legacy     17
Jackson Hatch: The Rise and Fall of a Public Man     21
Dr. Howard B. Gates & His Maybeck House     23
Albert Solon: Master Tile Artist     25
Carol Henning: The Girl From the Class of '24     27
Cora Older: Of Romance and Roses     29
Downtown Movie Memories     35
The Deluxe Theater: San Jose's First Movie Palace     39
Our Neighborhood Theaters     41
Our Binder and Curtis Buildings     43
Aestheticism Comes to San Jose     47
Our Craftsman Heritage     49
University of Pacific Legacy     51
The King Conservatory of Music/Germania Hall     55
San Jose's Forgotten Private Parks     57
The Alum Rock Park Log Cabin     59
East San Jose: City of 2,000 Days     61
The Smith House: An Evergreen Landmark     65
The William Wehner Estate     67
The Historic Almaden Winery     71
The Sainte Claire Hotel     75
New Life For The Medico-Dental Building     79
The De Anza Hotel     81
Down to the Station     85
Where is Washington Square     87
The San Jose Carnegie Library     89
The Pratt Home     93
St. James Square Historical District     95
The Sainte Claire Club     99
The Letcher Garage: Scene of Triumph and Tragedy     103
Camp Almaden: Our C.C.C. Outpost     105
Hot Springs Fever     107
Art and Connoisseurship in Early San Jose     109
A Tourist Guide History of San Jose and Environs     113
Santa Clara County Goes To The World's Columbian Exhibition: Chicago, 1893     117
The Great Race Comes to Town     121
San Jose Greets the Great White Fleet     125
The Great Bridge Disaster of 1917     129
The 1918 Flu Epidemic     133
The San Jose Round-up Days, 1915–1918     135
Renzel, Politics and Progress     139

# Introduction

## A MILLION STORIES...

BEING THE SON OF A JOURNALIST and brought up by a grandmother who had her feet firmly planted in the past, I have never been surprised that my interests gravitated toward research and writing about historical subjects. It was no coincidence that I chose to become a university librarian where such activities are the order of the day. My curiosity regarding the lives of ordinary citizens of earlier times, what is called social history, led me to explore our local situation with students in my New College seminars. Ideas from these experiences led to articles written for campus and local publications.

When Kathy Muller, Museum Association Administrator, asked me for copy for their *Association News*, I had a number of articles that could readily be reprinted in what would become our local history column: "Historical Footnotes of Santa Clara Valley." At first I worried that, once I'd run through my accumulated stock of material, I might have trouble coming up with ideas for future issues. This proved to be no problem, for my involvement with the San Jose Historical Landmarks Commission, the San Jose Historical Museum Development Council and later the Santa Clara County Historical Heritage Commission provided subjects for many pieces.

After the dissolution of San Jose State's New College program, I became curator of the University's John Steinbeck Research Center and later head of the Library's Special Collections Department, and this led to a number of articles on campus history and Steinbeck's connections with our area. My passion for the arts found an outlet in articles on our local arts institutions and their activities including music schools, movie theaters, and Senator Phelan's Montalvo.

Curiosity about how locals responded to great national events led to pieces on the 1918 flu epidemic, the arrival of Teddy Roosevelt's Great White Fleet, the 1908 New York to Paris car race and the impact of the Civilian Conservation Corps on our valley.

Digging through the records of the past to meet the next deadline invariably led to ideas for future stories. And on it goes—as the announcer for the old television series intoned: "there are a million stories in the naked city"—and so it seems for the Santa Clara Valley.

Early in the process Kathy Muller and I agreed that the accumulated material could become the basis for one of the Association's future membership premium books. So here you have almost a decade of writing about one of our favorite subjects—the Santa Clara Valley. It certainly is not the end of the trail for this writer. There is still the next deadline, and who knows, perhaps the "Son of Historical Footnotes."

*Jack Douglas*
*September 4, 1993*

# Acknowledgments

I would like to thank the following people who have helped me in my research and writing: Clyde and Helen Arbuckle, Marvin and Bonnie Bamburg, Dr. Charles Burdick, Riley Doty, Theron and Francis Fox, Mignon Gibson, April Halberstadt, Judi Henderson, Friedolin Kessler, Glory Ann Laffey; Pat Loomis, Leslie Masunaga, Gloria Pitman, Judy Stabile and Dr. James Walsh.

Special thanks to my editors of the column and the book: Kathy Muller and Carolyn Gagnon. Thanks also to my many colleagues in the libraries and historical research centers who have carefully maintained the records of our Valley's past so that each new generation might discover the richness of our heritage.

Jack Douglas

# Andrew Jackson Grayson - The Audubon Of The West

MUCH HAS BEEN WRITTEN ABOUT such San Jose pioneer artists as Andrew P. Hill and A.D.M. Cooper, but only recently has it come to light that another significant western painter began his artistic career here in the 1850s. Andrew Jackson Grayson's paintings of western birds have earned him the title of "The Audubon of the West."

From the beginning, Andrew Grayson, who was the son of a wealthy Louisiana planter, loved the wilderness. He spent his youth tramping the marshes of his native state and glorying in its abundant birdlife. His early attempts to become an artist were quashed by his practical father who persuaded his son to enter the mercantile profession. Well-educated for his time, Grayson graduated from a Catholic college near St. Louis. In 1842 he married Frances Jane Timmons, a Louisiana girl who shared many of his enthusiasms. Together they would lead an eventful life which they could scarcely have dreamt of early on.

Andrew, Frances and their baby son Edward became "overlanders" in 1846, passing over the Sierras only days before the ill-fated Donner Party. The same fate might have befallen their party had not Grayson, who was acting as leader, rushed ahead to secure help in the Sacramento Valley.

Andrew Jackson Grayson.

A true pioneer and a man of many talents, Grayson served as an officer in the Mexican War, worked the gold fields, operated a store in San Francisco and speculated in real estate. He established his first estate in Marin County near the present site of Fairfax. Like many other entrepreneurs in the turbulent West, he made and lost fortunes with equanimity. He took great pride in his role as an argonaut, and was a founding member of the Society of California Pioneers. According to Clyde Arbuckle's *History of San Jose*, Grayson paid the distinguished western artist William S. Jewett $2,000 in 1850 to paint "The Promised Land." This panoramic painting depicts Grayson, his wife and son, all in pioneer garb, descending from the Sierras into California. The painting, given to the San Francisco Mercantile Library, has become a classic of its kind.

An event occurred in 1852 that would permanently alter the course of Grayson's life. Frances Grayson chanced upon the recently acquired elephant folio edition of Audubon's *Birds of America* at the Mercantile Library. Remembering her husband's early interest in bird drawing, Frances wasted no time in bringing this find to his attention. Grayson was enthralled by the color and detail in the works of his fellow Louisianan. It reminded him of his childhood ambition and inspired him to do for the West what Audubon had done for the eastern United States. In so doing he would give up his business, much of his family life, and ultimately, his own life in the pursuit of a career as an artist-ornithologist.

Leaving his business interests in other hands, Grayson decided that the South Bay was the best place to observe and paint birdlife. In 1853 he purchased four acres of land in San Jose near Julian and Fourth Streets from a Mr. Quivvey, and established a studio there which he called Bird's Nest Cottage. The Graysons surrounded their cottage with a variety of plants and shrubs, making the place something of an attraction in San Jose. As he wrote in his journal: *In a beautiful spot nestling among the trees and roses was our delightful little cottage, with its artesian well in the front yard, a perpetual flowing fountain of crystal water. Tame birds ran about the yard which had been domesticated with much care and skill. Wild ones sang in the grove about the house. It was a spot everyone delighted to visit.* His son Edward attended the Santa Clara Mission School.

In this state of rural bliss Grayson began to revive his repressed talents as an artist. Having no formal training in art, Grayson tried as best he could to follow the example of the great Audubon in capturing the postures of the birds perched and in flight. One of his earliest subjects was a tame roadrunner which he used for close observation. Like Audubon, Grayson wrote accompanying "biographies" of each of the species he sketched, describing in detail the bird's

manners and habitats. Of the roadrunner he wrote: *The roadrunner is seldom seen in trees, unless pursued very closely, when it has been seen to spring from the ground to the branches, at a height of ten or fifteen feet at a single bound, but prefers running along a road or path, from whence it derives its name. I have now in my possession one of these birds, which is becoming quite tame, and readily feeds upon any kind of raw meat, but prefers lizards and small birds, which it swallows whole - feathers and all. If they are given to him alive, he will play with them awhile before swallowing them, just as a cat will do with a mouse. I have seen him devour three sparrows, one lizard and a portion of the breast of a coot for his breakfast without experiencing apparent inconvenience.*

The house finch became another of his favorite subjects: *A pair of these birds built their nest in a small bush in my garden in San Jose, the young of which I placed in a cage, just before they were able to fly, and removed them to the house. The old ones followed and still continued to feed them through the bars of their little prison. I soon took pity on them, however, and gave them their freedom.*

Soon Grayson's drawings and articles began to appear in such publications as the *Hesperian*, the *Hutching's California Magazine*, and the *California Farmer and Journal of Useful Science*. A friend persuaded him to enter his work at the California State Fair in 1855. His paintings of the Caribbean red-billed tropic bird, the wood duck and his pet, the California roadrunner, were awarded the first prize and a silver cup. Entries in the San Jose fair the following year also took first prizes.

As Grayson's artistic skill increased, he became more aware of the inadequacy of his scientific knowledge. Realizing that if he was to follow in the steps of Audubon he would need some formal training in ornithology, he wrote to the Smithsonian Institution for advice. Thus he began a fruitful correspondence with Spencer Fullerton Baird, the man who was to become this country's leading 19th century ornithologist. Baird gave Grayson what might be called an extended correspondence course in ornithology. Grayson in turn sent many preserved specimens of western birds to the Smithsonian where they formed a nucleus of that institution's bird collection. Grayson would be the last of the self-educated naturalists such as Audubon who, if not college trained biologists, had the advantage of seeing wildlife in its natural habitat before the onslaught of civilization.

*The* Lesser Roadrunner *from* Birds of the Pacific Slope, *a portfolio of 156 Bird Portraits by Andrew Jackson Grayson, San Jose State University Library Special Collections.*

Baird, who valued the texts of the great Audubon's work above the masterly drawings, encouraged Grayson's focus on the delineations of the habits and peculiarities of the species he encountered. We have, for example, from Grayson's notes the earliest warnings of the decline of the California condor: *In the early days of California history, it was more frequently met with than now. Being of a cautious and shy disposition, the rapid settlement of the country has partially driven it off to more secluded localities.* Baird was not to comprehend the magnitude of Grayson's artistic talent until some years after the painter's death.

Grayson was not content to remain in the comfortable surroundings of Bird's Nest Cottage. He wrote: *We sat under our vines and fig trees, and ate apples, peaches and strawberries of our own raising. But were we happy? Did all this bright anticipation, after we had tasted the fruits of reality, bring us contentment? No siree! ... And in December 1856 we sold everything but the house and grounds, which I mortgaged and leased to the original owner, Mr. Quivvey. I determined to leave California for aye! The land which I went to poor and almost destitute, became rich and left poor again. Such are the ups and downs of life. ... My destination was Tehuantepec. I sent my son to St. James College in Maryland to school on the 19th of January 1857. And on the 17th of March following we found ourselves embarked on the* Mary Taylor *for Tehuantepec.*

Grayson left the serenity of his home in San Jose for a life that would be fraught with danger, hardship and ultimate tragedy. The ship *Mary Taylor* was wrecked while landing and the Graysons lost most of their belongings, including a portfolio of paintings. In less than a year, a bout of fever (Grayson's) made a return to the Bay Area necessary. In 1859 the Graysons returned to Mexico, this time to Mazatlan. From this base Grayson painted the majority of the pictures on which his reputation rests.

It was always Grayson's dream to have his works published in a manner similar to the great Audubon folios. In 1866 he was received by the Emperor Maximilian and Empress Carlota who assured them that the National Academy would subsidize the printing of a folio complete with hand colored plates and text in English, French and Spanish. The overthrow and execution of Maximilian brought an end to these plans.

A personal tragedy of great magnitude occurred when the artist's 25 year old son was mysteriously murdered while accompanying his father on one of his explorations in 1867. Undaunted, in spite of his deep sorrow, Grayson continued his painting and study, driven on by the variety and richness of the avian population along the coast of Mexico. On a trip to Isabel Island aboard the *U.S.S. Mohongo,* Grayson was stricken with a fever which resulted in his death.

He died in Mazatlan on August 17, 1869, a few days short of his 50th birthday.

Following her husband's wishes, Frances Grayson tried for ten years to interest various groups in publishing his manuscript entitled: *The Birds of the Pacific Slope.* She even sent the paintings to Philadelphia for the Centennial of 1876, hoping that they might attract a publisher. Finding no one willing to take on the publication, she decided finally to give the paintings to the University of California. Upon her death in 1909, all of her scrapbooks and other Grayson material were also given to the University.

For over a century the works of the "Audubon of the West" lay in the archives of the Bancroft Library, forgotten to all but a few. In 1982 they were brought to the attention of Andrew Hoyem, one of the nation's leading creators of fine crafted books. He saw the immediate need to bring Grayson's work before a larger audience. Hoyem, through his Arion Press, spared no expense in reproducing the *Birds of the Pacific Slope* in a folio limited edition of 156 bird portraits along with an accompanying volume of Grayson's field notes and a biography of the artist by Lois C. Stone. This splendid publication compares favorably with the priceless Audubon folios. The San Jose State University Library has acquired this magnificent set for our community.

# The Loves and Trials of Brigadier General Henry M. Naglee

Geneneral Henry Morris Naglee, for whom a San Jose street and neighborhood are named, is generally considered one of our most distinguished early citizens. A graduate of West Point, he served in the Mexican War and the Civil War. Upon settling in San Jose after his war service, Naglee became a pioneer viticulturist, and produced the much lauded Naglee Brandy. Alum Rock Park was established largely through his efforts and it was he who planted the avenue of trees which led to the park.

There was a period, however, when the Naglee name was not so hallowed, a period when the General's relations with two women became a public scandal. Both incidents centered around alleged breach of promise to marry situations.

The first began innocently enough when Naglee, for reasons of health, decided in 1858 to leave his thriving banking business in San Francisco and settle into the life of a country squire in San Jose. At a private party prior to Christmas of that year he met and became enamored of a young San Francisco woman named Mary Schell. It is uncertain whether or not he had genuine intentions of marrying Miss Schell; Naglee put off the decision and took a long journey to Europe in 1860 to study viticulture and to bring back vines to be cultivated on his San Jose farm.

He returned to San Jose only briefly before leaving again by steamer for the east coast to join the Union Forces. As a Brigadier General in the Army, he distinguished himself as a leader in the early battles. A hero at the Battle of Fair Oaks (May 1862), he was seriously wounded while leading his troops.

It would be four years before he would see his "beloved" Mary again. During this time he kept up a correspondence with her which suggested in the most intimate terms his desire for her. Mary Schell was to be deeply disappointed, however, when upon his return in early 1865, Naglee gave her a cold and abrupt dismissal.

The wounded Miss Schell, who had waited over six years for her "Harry," considered for a time taking the General to court, but her desire for vengeance took a much more creative turn. Mary

*General Naglee*

simply gathered up a collection of some of the General's more intimate and potentially embarrassing letters and had them published by a firm in San Francisco. The volume, which appeared in 1867, was entitled: *The Love Life of Brigadier General Henry M. Naglee, Consisting of a Correspondence on Love, War and Politics.*

The introduction to the book, penned by an anonymous editor in a style which resembled that of a Mark Twain or Ambrose Bierce, was an attempt to exonerate Mary for the publication of the letters by claiming that:

*It was with a struggle she consented to have them made public, and then only when it became imperative for her to defend herself from the calumnies of purchased miscreants.*

*She has endured poverty, reproach and privation, rather than compromise the reputation of the man she loved, notwithstanding their publication would have secured her ample means, and this too while the 'amatory penman' was rioting in the enjoyment of superabundant wealth. Yet these tender missives remained locked in secret, bedewed mayhap with many a tear, while Slander sent its hydra hiss abroad, and the faithless hero mocked at the ruin he had caused.*

Not wishing to miss an opportunity to skewer his subject, the editor attempts to apologize for Naglee's writing style: *"Of the letters themselves, viewed with the most good natured eye, and bearing in mind the fact that heroes are not always remarkable for their intelligence, we must admit that they are by no means of a classic style of literature."* Finally the editor states: *"Others (letters) trench upon more subdued scenes, having in them much that is ludicrous, while all are seasoned with a 'passionate' flavor that cannot fail to tickle the palate of the most sensational epicure."*

The editor is correct about Naglee's writing style, but historians and some of us not perhaps so high minded owe a debt to Mary Schell for making the letters public. Written in a personal style by a figure who had a leading role in our nation's history, these unique documents are revealing in their insight into events and attitudes of the time.

This rare volume, which has only recently been added to the collection of San Jose State University's Special Collections Department, has far too many choice bits to be included in an essay of this length, however, I have tried to select those that are the most representative.

Naglee was in his mid-forties when he first met Mary Schell. One can only surmise that his active business life had kept him from earlier marriage or perhaps there were few women in the West who met the genteel standards of the Philadelphia society in which he was raised. At the time he was courting Miss Schell, he wrote his friend George Ringgold that he was afraid he would never find a woman attractive enough to marry.

Perhaps Mary became more precious to him at a distance than close at hand. Throughout the wartime separation he wrote to her suggesting that her love alone kept him alive through all the horrors of war and politics on the Potomac. His letters, always addressed to his 'Chere Petite,' 'Dear dear baby,' 'My own dear, darling little one,' may lead the reader to assume that Miss Schell was rather slight in stature. Be that as it may, he poured out his longings like a lovesick schoolboy:

*I hardly know what to say. I have absolutely nothing to tell you, except only that I love you constantly; that I have the most intense desire to see and be with you, to make you, if possible, more excessively happy than ever. I want again to feel that sweet, dear little heart against mine, and to hear you once breathe, in flattering words: Dear, dear darling Harry, how very, very, excessively, excessively happy we are; we were made for each other.*

One can understand why Mary waited so long for her 'Harry' with such encouragement as the following:

*Dear Baby, are we not well mated? Was ever man and woman more completely so? Have we not loved, and loved and grown lean and fattened on love? Have we not whispered love with all its sweetest accents, unintelligible but to the very, very few that have loved as we have loved?*

And later in some reference to a rumor about his character:

*I love you, dear Baby! and oh, how intensely! one only equal to the intensity of my love would be my misery, and pain, and suffering, if my love was for one moment forgotten. Live on, love on, my dear one; listen not to bad counsels, it matters not from whom they come, but let the past remind you that the world is but a passing dream, and that you can rely on almost no one. Who has been to you always, from the first moment you first knew him, as faithful, as watchful, as truly devoted to you, as your own Harry?*

*And who, in your cool judgment, will you believe will last and watch over you always, let what will occur, as he has done and will do? ... I feel that you are devotedly, exclusively, wholly mine, body and soul, mind and thought, night and day, and every hour of the day.*

Perhaps because of the difference in their ages or the custom of the times, the General wrote to his 'Baby' in a most patronizing and paternalistic way, advising her on personal manners and on behavior:

*My dear Love, let me ask you to have some employment always near you. You can sew; you can knit; you can practice your piano — do anything; but do not find yourself idle. ... You see Love, how much of Christian goodness I can advise; and when near you, or when my thoughts are engaged in your welfare, it has always been thus.*

One of his most bizarre recommendations, considering the Victorian morals of the day, was on the importance of physical exercise. He describes how he has learned to do pushups on the edge of his bathtub after bathing:

*I commenced with doing this half a dozen times, and could do no more; now I do so twenty times. I do so every morning, arms are double the size they were a month ago. I would like to see you try it - not in your tub, for it is too small.*

Congratulating himself for his achievement, Naglee goes on to say:

*I had not discovered, when I recommended the tub so strongly, the grand combination tub, uniting the gymnastic exercise with bathing. The inventive genius of the Yankee nation is truly astonishing and unlimited.*

As if his descriptions were not explicit enough, the General drew a picture of himself poised naked on the rim of his tub. The editor of the letters devoted a full page to a reproduction of this drawing.

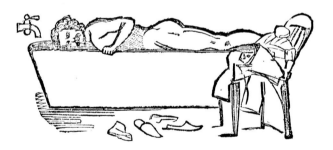

*Pen & Ink sketch, as drawn by himself.*

That the General could be jealous and vindictive was expressed in a letter from Philadelphia shortly after his mother's death:

*I would rather lose every relative there remains to me than to have you go wrong. I would rather the fires of Hell should enter your brain and breath than that man should near your lips or touch your hand; and should this*

*happen, from thence and forever stop all communication with me.*

Naglee was a Democrat, and found it difficult to function under Lincoln's Republican regime. He most resented any attempts to "abolitionize the war."

*Nine-tenths of the Northern people are against the fanatics (abolitionists), and they would not permit any attempt at any negro insurrection; besides, it has been demonstrated in the late Harper's Ferry affair that negroes won't go against their masters. I am disgusted with the outrageous interference of politicians in the conduct of the war. They are determined to introduce abolition into the war, and make officers of the army aid them in their hellish purpose.*

Naglee, whose imperious nature led to a long history of clashes with his superior officers, found it difficult to serve under generals whom he considered his intellectual inferiors. Of General Hooker, his division commander, he states:

*...one of my troubles comes from the fact that Hooker is inefficient; he is slow and not capable...I am too strong for him. My opinions receive favor in Washington to the condemnation of his plans.*

Though a proven and fearless leader in battle, General Naglee was denied the promotion he had earned, and summed up his situation well in the following statement:

*I have the reputation of being a thorough soldier, and could I only have played the hypocrite, and upheld the negro government, I could have been very prominent in the Army. But, Baby, I not only could not do that, but I could not and would not conceal my utter abhorrence and disgust; the result of which is, that I have been incessantly persecuted. I love opposition; there is excitement in it.*

When Mary's little bombshell struck, more than a few top army officers must have felt the blast. Naglee damned most of them with such remarks as:

*I say that Keyes is as much out of his ele-*

*ment as that noted hen that sat upon duck's eggs, and in my estimation is much more chicken hearted - infinitely more selfish. Enough of him!*

*Thank God, I am now entirely beyond his influence, and whilst his star is in the mud, mine slowly ascends, and will shine when Keyes, Hooker, Heintzelman and Peck — all made by stealing my credit — are forgotten. These men with McDowell, Sumner and others, have got beyond their depth. By slow degrees, truth will out and justice will be done.*

To Naglee's credit, one must remember that Lincoln himself had many of the same misgivings about his generals.

Naglee's candor caused him to be relieved of a command and shifted back and forth among several military departments. In 1864, he abruptly left the Army before the war's end, but stayed in Washington long enough to support General George McClellen, the Democratic candidate for President, who ran against Lincoln.

Did Naglee, upon his return to San Francisco, find Mary a pale reflection of the vision he had had on the battlefields, or did he sense that his jealous and possessive fears about her were justified? His final letter seems to imply that she had not been all together true to her 'Harry:'

*My Dear Friend: I have been quite unwell since my arrival, but not ill enough to be confined to my room. I have not called again, for the reason that I have no intention to interrupt any of your friendly associations so agreeably established. I shall always be most happy to know that you are doing well.*

There is no question that the publication of these letters was an embarrassment to the General, especially as regards his acquaintances in the East. Even more damaging to his reputation, however, were the subsequent breach of promise and perjury suits brought a decade later by another young woman by the name of Emily Hanks.

In the mid-1870s the residents of the sleepy town of San Jose were scandalized by a breach of promise suit brought against General Henry M. Naglee by his children's former governess, Emily Hanks. The second trial, the result of Naglee's

*Naglee Monument in St. James Park.*
*Photo by Jack Douglas.*

appeal, caused a further sensation.

At age fifty, after a lifetime of accumulating wealth through banking and real estate and time out for stints in the Mexican and Civil Wars, the General had to think seriously about marriage and heirs. So, shortly after the Mary Schell affair he became engaged to Marie Antoinette Ringgold, the eighteen year old daughter of an old military colleague. Not only was Marie virginal (she was considering becoming a nun), she was also descended from James Monroe, the fifth President of the U.S.

Within a year of their marriage a daughter, Marie, was born. A second daughter, Antoinette, was born in 1869, but the fragile mother died in childbirth. Naglee then had to resort to employing nursemaids to care for the children, and that is how Emily Hanks arrived on the scene in 1871.

Emily, a local girl whose mother was Spanish, had attended school until she was seventeen and thereafter did sewing work for various families in town. She was 21 when Naglee hired her as a live-in nursemaid at a wage of $50 per month. She performed her duties as nurse, governess and housekeeper until February 1875, when she had an argument over her wages (a continual sore point) and left the General's house.

Emily fled to the neighboring Collins residence at 10th and Santa Clara. She had gotten to know Mrs. Collins whose husband was the flamboyant attorney W. H. Collins. (Collins had, that same year, unsuccessfully defended the bandit Tiburcio Vasquez.) There was no love lost between Naglee and Collins, so it is not surprising that Collins took Emily in for a stay of two months and became her legal advisor.

Collins made arrangements through Naglee's attorney, D.M. Delmas, to settle Emily's back wages and find her employment at the U.S. Mint in San Francisco. J.J. Owen, owner of the *Mercury* served as an adjudicator in these transactions.

Naglee, seemingly, had not lost interest in Emily. He visited her in San Francisco and wrote numerous letters asking her to return. Emily did visit sporadically and then moved back in July 1875.

In August Emily announced that she was pregnant and demanded that the General marry her. Naglee refused and when the situation became untenable he made her leave. He did, however, at the urging of her doctor, pay for her medical care during the final stages of her pregnancy and for the birth.

Emily filed a breach of promise suit, claiming that on June 5, 1875 the General had proposed marriage and, after her acceptance, seduced her. The trial was heard in the spring of 1877, Superior Court Judge David Beldon presiding. The proceedings were the talk of the town, and Naglee's attorneys would claim in their appeal that "the jury was under the influence of passion and prejudice." Naglee, who testified that he had never had intimate relations with Miss Hanks, never-the-less lost the case. The jury ruled in her favor and awarded damages of $27,500 (she had asked for $30,000). The *San Jose Herald* of May 31 took the moral high ground in the following editorial:

## Hanks-Naglee Breach of Promise Case and its Lessons

*We refrained from publishing the proceedings of the late trial in which Emily Hanks was plaintiff, and General Henry M. Naglee was defendant, because we thought public decency would be wounded rather than benefitted by their recital. But now the trial is ended, and the result, with its lessons, belongs to the public.*

*In many of its features the case was a remarkable one, and had it been tried in San Francisco, the sensation journals of that metropolis would have been loaded to the guards, during the seven days of the trial, with its disgusting details. The parties to the action - the plaintiff, a poor and obscure country girl, an orphan, and friendless; the defendant, a titled millionaire living in luxury at his home in San Jose, fairer and more Eden-like than the island of Blennerhassett, with princely income flowing in from his dozen estates in as many counties - the large amount of the damages claimed - the very able counsel employed on either side, and the deep and throbbing interest which every one felt in the result, all combined to make the trial the most memorable which has ever engaged the attention of our local courts. Without prejudice on the one side or partiality on the other, we deem it our duty, as faithful journalists, to point the lessons which have been taught by this long-to-be-remembered law suit.*

*First then, let us note that public morals which for years have been outraged by a notorious and disgraceful liaison have now been avenged by the magnitude of the verdict of an honest jury, representing our society in one of its supremest moments. Arrogant wealth has been taught that there is a limit to its immunities; and hereafter, in this community at least, it will not be likely to indulge the false dream that its circle is charmed, and that its unchaste orgies will not be broken in upon by the swift messengers of violated and down-trodden law. The aegis of a healthy public sentiment has been interposed between the unprotected orphan and the gray-headed libertine who looked upon her as his powerless victim. Her very weakness under the protection of that sentiment has been the weapon of power under the blows of which her betrayer has fallen. Those who are without shame, and who ignore or laugh at the frowns of a society outraged by their indecent and scandalous manner of life, are here taught that they can at least be compelled to disgorge a part of the wealth which they fondly imagine is their security and protection. We contemplate with pride the proof furnished by the verdict of a Santa Clara county jury, that an unprotected and friendless girl, in a just cause, is more than a match for all the strength and power which wealth can command. And we are most glad to know that by this verdict the seducer of innocence has been admonished that he will invoke in vain, as a defense of his crime, the degraded condition to which his own lusts have reduced his victim.*

*We can offer no apology for the conduct of the plaintiff. The disclosures of the trial show but too plainly her folly, her weakness, and her fatal fall before the blandishments of her seducer, and the glitter of his riches. The money she acquires by this verdict will be but poor compensation for the jewel of innocence which she surrendered, the loss of her woman's honor, and the death of her good name. It will console her but little as, with her disgraced child, who treads the dark ways of the future, whose shadows are already falling thick around her. We pity her in her shame and degradation, but we reprobate, beyond the language at our command, the wretch whose stronger nature, aided by the display of his wealth and surroundings of splendor, has wrought her ruin. He has blighted two lives by his hellish licentiousness, and society should keep faithful vigil to protect its citadels of virtue from the approach of this slayer of innocence and robber of chastity. All decent people would rather welcome pestilence and death than permit that moral leper to cross the threshold of their home.*

This must certainly have been the General's darkest hour. But the hero of the Battle of Seven Pines, whose horse was shot out from under him, was not ready to surrender.

Naglee's attorneys filed for an appeal which was denied by Judge Beldon. Not deterred, they filed for and were granted an appeal by the State Supreme Court. The subsequent trial in 1879 brought more of the truth to light.

Witnesses and letters were presented which cast doubt on Emily Hanks' truthfulness. Dr. A.J. Spencer, the family doctor, testified that Emily had been the General's mistress as early as 1871. The General gave testimony on the details of their "life of sin," including his method for safe sex. Naglee's lawyers, using every device to strip away Emily's guise of naive innocence, traced all of her actions of the days when she conceived the child, thereby building a somewhat convincing argument that she was having an affair with William Collins — a likely candidate for father of her child.

The lawyers hoped that, by blackening Emily Hanks' reputation, they would be able to, at the least, make a case for decrease of the damages awarded. They needn't have worried, for the court determined that there wasn't a preponderance of evidence that a marriage proposal had been made. The General was off the hook financially if not morally.

Emily didn't give up. She initiated proceedings to convict the General of perjury during the first trial, but because his perjured testimony was not considered relevant to the breach of promise, her suit was dismissed.

By now people were tired of the case and even the *Herald* published, on May 7, 1880, an editorial that might be considered a retraction of their earlier fulminations:

### A Protest Against Prejudice

*The Hanks-Naglee case, tried some three years ago, in which the expectations of the plaintiff were frustrated by the decision of the Supreme Court, has assumed a new phase, as a criminal suit for perjury, which is entirely unjustifiable, and which cannot result in any possible public good.*

*From our own knowledge of the case we should say that General Naglee did no more than was right in appealing to the Supreme Court, and as to the use of any improper influences on his part, on the part of the Supreme Court, no one but a prejudiced person would ever have thought of such a thing. The only surprise that we ever heard expressed being that the grounds taken by the Supreme Court for the reversal of the case, were not discovered by the Court below.*

*We protest against any attempt to prejudge the case by improper means. General Naglee is one of our most enterprising citizens, entitled to a fair and impartial hearing, which is all that he would ask for. We not only make this protest in this connection, but wish to be understood as condemning any and all attempts to try causes in the newspapers before they reach the courts.*

The transcript of the second trial reads like a soap opera. It is an insightful document that describes the everyday life of an early San Jose and its definable class system.

The letters of the two protagonists which were entered as evidence show that, at one time, they had felt genuine affection for each other and for the Naglee children. Naglee continued to entreat her favors up until she filed suit. One can only assume that he would not consider marriage because he considered her beneath his station.

Emily Hanks had spunk and one would like to think that she and her child got on well in the world. (Contrary to the *Herald* editorial, she did have relatives.) The records seem to be silent about her fate.

The General died six years later at the Occidental Hotel in San Francisco. His name was conspicuously absent from all local histories until 1915 when his daughters erected the monument to him which stands in St. James Park.

# Sarah Knox-Goodrich

SARAH KNOX-GOODRICH IS REMEMBERED TODAY, if she is remembered at all, for the charming three-story Romanesque storefront on South First Street. Constructed in 1889 at her direction, the building bears the delicately carved monogram K G in the sandstone pediment above the third floor windows.

Sarah was the widow of two of the county's most wealthy and prominent men: Dr. William Knox, a financier and legislator, and architect Levi Goodrich who designed many of our civic monuments, including the county courthouse, old city hall and the state normal school. It is possible that, as a loving wife to both, Sarah meant the building as a memorial to them, but given the fact that this proud and independent woman was a California Pioneer, a community organizer, and a national leader for women's suffrage, perhaps we should consider the building a memorial to her as well.

*From Munro-Fraser,* History of Santa Clara County.

Born Sarah Louise Browning in Culpepper County, Virginia in 1827, she was the daughter of a farmer whose chief claim to fame was having served as a private in the War of 1812. The family moved to Missouri when Sarah was eleven. When she was nineteen she met and married William Knox. Knox was a Tennessean who had graduated from the University of Kentucky, and after the marriage the couple went back to the university where he obtained a medical degree.

After practicing medicine for several years in Missouri, Knox made the decision to take his family, which now included baby daughter Virginia, on a wagon train to California. Sarah and her sister-in-law, Virginia Knox, were the only women in the party. They arrived, after a six month journey, in Nevada City on October 8, 1850.

Knox practiced medicine but found the proprietorship of the South Yuba Canal Company much more profitable. The canal, which stretched to the north for several hundred miles, brought the much needed water to the gold mining operations around Nevada City. Dr. Knox also took time from his busy life to serve in the California Assembly.

Tiring of the rough and ready lifestyle of the mining towns, and perhaps looking for a stable place to invest his earnings, Knox brought his family to San Jose in 1863. Here with his brother-in-law T. Ellard Beans he established the city's first bank, the Bank of San Jose which was located on the southeast corner of Santa Clara and First. He chose architect Levi Goodrich to design and oversee the construction of this building and that of the Knox Block, a large office building on the northwest corner of the same intersection. Goodrich, in turn, chose the Knox Block as the permanent address for his thriving firm.

Dr. Knox rejoined the legislature in 1865, this time as senator from Santa Clara County. Sarah was by then concerned with the rights of women and was instrumental in having her husband introduce a bill to allow married women to dispose of their estates by will without the consent of their husbands. Knox did not serve long in the Senate, for he died in November,

1867, leaving Sarah a very wealthy woman.

Sarah, whose daughter was soon to marry, threw much of her subsequent efforts into working for women's rights. She founded the San Jose Women's Suffrage Association in 1869 and rapidly became a leader in state and national circles. Guests at her palatial home on North First Street included Susan B. Anthony and Elizabeth Cady Stanton. In tactics which sound familiar today, Sarah refused to pay her considerable taxes without "representation." As a gesture, she frequently offered her vote in elections in order to have it publicly refused. To quote from Stanton's *History of Women's Suffrage: The county suffrage society has had an untiring leader in Mrs. Goodrich, and on all occasions she has nerved the weak and encouraged the timid by her example of unflinching devotion.*

The Knox-Goodrich building as it looked recently. Photo by Charles Shields.

The nation's centennial in 1876 provided a fine opportunity for Sarah. Perceiving that the suffragettes would not be welcome in the 4th of July parade, and knowing that the parade would pass by two sides of her house, she surrounded the house with such painted slogans as: WE ARE DENIED THE BALLOT BUT COMPELLED TO PAY TAXES, and, TAXATION WITHOUT REPRESENTATION IS A TYRANNY AS MUCH IN 1876 AS IT WAS IN 1776, and, GOVERNMENTS DERIVE THEIR JUST POWERS FROM THE CONSENT OF THE GOVERNED. When the suffragettes were, after all, allowed to join the parade, Sarah requested that they be placed between the blacks and the Chinese in order to emphasize the fact that these recently emancipated and enfranchised groups had more rights than women.

She spoke before the California Legislature on numerous occasions, and helped, in spite of almost universal opposition from local legislators, to pass a bill which would give women the right to hold educational offices. She also carried on a long and costly legal battle with the government to see that her aged mother received her Veterans of the War of 1812 widow's pension.

Fourteen years after the death of her first hus-

band, Sarah married Levi Goodrich. The ceremony took place in her home, solemnized by Reverend Dr. W.W. McKaig and attended by a few family friends. One, Mr. T.C. Park congratulated the bride "on having a Goodrich husband," and the bridegroom "on having a *good rich* wife."

Levi, who was now leaving more of the architectural business to his son Edwin, became increasingly involved in his sandstone quarry which was located off of Almaden Road in South San Jose. It was from this quarry that the stone for most of the Bay area's public buildings was cut. The stone was used for Stanford University and, of course, for the Knox-Goodrich building.

In 1887, while visiting San Diego with Sarah (there were many Goodrich buildings there as well), Levi died suddenly of apoplexy. Another family tragedy occurred on July 6, 1903; Levi's son Edwin was killed when an Alum Rock trolley on which he was a passenger rolled out of control down a steep grade and overturned. Sarah herself fell ill a few months later, and in spite of the ministrations of her daughter and Dr. Howard B. Gates, she died of gastritis on October 30, 1903. She was buried between her husbands in the family plot in Oak Hill Cemetery.

Carved monogram in the pediment above the third floor windows of the Knox-Goodrich building. Photo by Charles Shields.

*Mary Hayes-Chynoweth*
*San Jose Historical Museum Collections*

# Mary Hayes-Chynoweth

MARY HAYES-CHYNOWETH IS REMEMBERED TODAY primarily for the mansion that bears the family name. This mansion, located in Edenvale, was built in 1905, and was for years the residence of the Hayes clan, one of the region's most powerful families. The Hayes brothers owned the *San Jose Mercury* and the *News* from which, early in the century, they editorialized against San Jose's corrupt city politics. Everis Hayes was, for seven terms, an influential U.S. Congressman, and his brother, Jay Orley, ran unsuccessfully for Governor in 1918. The matriarch, Mary Folsom Hayes-Chynoweth, was, however, the driving force in the family. A preacher, faith healer and nationally known spiritualist, she was one of the most fascinating American women of the nineteenth century.

Born in Holland, New York on October 2, 1825, Mary was the ninth child of Abraham and Miriam Folsom. Folsom, a blacksmith by trade, was an ordained Freewill Baptist minister by vocation. Mary, a particularly resourceful child, quickly learned many household skills, and since she had few opportunities to attend school, was primarily self-taught. As early as age eleven she showed an instinctual knowledge of herbal medicine which she utilized successfully on family and friends. With some coaching from her schoolmaster brother, Mary qualified to become a teacher herself at the age of seventeen. In 1850 she moved with her family to Waterloo, Wisconsin where she continued to teach.

Though at first skeptical of the great wave of spiritualism that was sweeping the country in the 1850s, Mary was to have second thoughts on the subject when one of her pupils, Cora Scott, began to manifest the ability to communicate with the dead through trances in which she wrote messages from deceased relatives. Cora soon went on the road with her talents and eventually became one of the nation's leading spiritualists.

Mary, feeling the need of divine guidance, went into a period of intense prayer and meditation. In a spell of extreme agitation she began speaking in tongues. She wrote: *the Power lifted me from my knees, took Father's Bible and turned to a page down which it pointed my finger and motioned my father to read aloud the section which states what the Apostles were appointed to do, to preach, to heal, to cast out devils, to speak with tongues!* It was Mary's belief from this day on that the "Power" was the Holy Spirit itself. Soon she was communicating telepathically and healing with the laying on of hands.

At the age of 29, Mary Folsom, ex-teacher and full-time faith healing preacher, must have felt that she was destined never to marry. All that changed when she met Anson Hayes. Hayes, a widowed well-to-do farmer, and cousin of President Rutherford B. Hayes, had been much impressed by Mary's sermons, and soon convinced her that marriage would not stand in the way of her "mission." Mary bore Anson three sons: Everis, Jay Orley and Carrol. Carrol was not to live beyond infancy.

The Hayes family made their first trip to California in 1872, hoping to find a better climate for Anson's failing health. They soon returned to Madison, Wisconsin were Anson died of a heart attack. Everis and Jay attended the University of Wisconsin where they received degrees in law. While in Madison, Mary was brought in to cure a Miss Ellen Chynoweth, who had been declared incurable by her physicians. Mary brought Ellen back to health, and the two families became life-long friends.

Everis and Jay prospered in the legal profession and soon began investing in real estate. Mary, who had moved in with them to keep house, was soon using her psychic powers to advise them on where to invest their money. At first, the boys balked at their mother's interference in their financial affairs, but Mary's acuity and persistence convinced them to follow her advice. Through spiritual revelation, Mary perceived that iron ore, not timber, was the source of big profits. She allegedly used her telepathic powers to help her sons buy a controlling interest in the unproductive Ashland Mine which all the experts had predicted would never produce iron ore. The "Power" advised Mary at each step of the way to finding the elusive ore. Like a water witcher Mary led the engi-

neers to the best veins. The "Power" then advised them to expand their operations to another site which became the Germania mine. The Ashland and Germania mines soon became two of the most productive sources of ore on the Great Lakes.

With their amassed wealth, Mary's "Power" advised her to move the family to California. In 1887, the Hayes and Chynoweth families traveled through the state, and they ultimately decided to settle on 240 acres in the Edenvale area. The land, once a part of the Bernal Rancho, was owned by John Tennant. The Tennant House, a spacious Victorian, was to be the first Hayes home while work proceeded on a more properly opulent dwelling.

The first Hayes Mansion, completed in 1891, was a storybook Victorian structure with a wide assortment of turrets, cupolas, balconies and bays. After the mansion's destruction, the *San Jose Mercury* described it as follows:

*The cost was $175,000. It was in all its appointments unapproached by any other private residence in the county. It was supplied with all the modern conveniences and had fifty rooms besides halls, cellars, bath-rooms and pantries.*

*It was lighted throughout solely by electricity supplied by a powerful dynamo and storage batteries. It was furnished throughout the greater portion with elaborate Eastern hardwood finish, put together in the same manner and finished and polished as nicely as any first class furniture. Artistic frescoes decorated the walls of some apartments, while in others they were covered entirely by hardwood paneling, and in others by tapestries, stamped leather and lincrusta waltons. The furniture was the most expensive anywhere.*

No expense was spared on the grounds which were designed by Mr. Ulrich who had made his name landscaping the famous Del Monte Hotel in Monterey. Many of the specimen trees still stand in the undeveloped area that once held Frontier Village Amusement Park. The Hayes' also built a $10,000 stable to house the thirty horses and forty mules needed for transportation and working the estate. A chapel made from sandstone from the Goodrich quarry was later added.

As always, the ever watchful and caring Mary looked after the welfare of the workers and surrounding neighbors. She constructed a school and library. The Tennant house became a residence for some of her many patients. One such patient was T.B. Chynoweth, an attorney and member of the family

*The first Hayes Mansion, built in 1891. From* Sunshine, Fruit & Flowers.

who came with the Hayes' to Edenvale. Suffering from near blindness, Mary returned T.B.'s sight and won his heart. Mary's first marriage had been to a man much older than herself; she was now being wooed by a man 21 years her junior.

The "Power" must have given her a green light, for in July 1890 she married T.B. Chynoweth in a double ceremony which included the groom's younger brother and the bride's niece. If there were any anxieties on the part of Mary's sons, they were soon alleviated, for T.B. died of apoplexy ten months after the wedding.

Mary took up her healing in even greater earnest after her husband's death. Her register indicates that she gave, in a period of two years, over 7,000 personal treatments, in addition to the numerous healings done by mail. She had to stand helplessly by, however, as her daughter-in-law Nettie lay dying. Nettie's doctors claimed that she was simply pregnant, but Mary told them that Nettie was afflicted with three tumors.

After Nettie's death, the autopsy indicated that she indeed had had three tumors.

Not all was well at the mines either. A disastrous fire envcloped the Germania mine (perhaps a portent of other fires that would plague the Hayes family), and it remained uncontrollable by any means known to the experts. Mary rushed to the scene to inform the men that if they were obedient and faithful, they would succeed in putting out the fire without a single injury. They struggled for five days while she paced the surface in prayer. The men accomplished feats under incredible conditions, and in the end, as Mary predicted, the fire was put out with no one harmed.

The economic crash of 1893 caused the family to lose control of the mines, and ultimately they had to mortgage the Edenvale estate. Once again, Mary was credited with making decisions that brought the family back to prosperity. Unfortunately in 1899, shortly after the mansion had been saved from the creditors, a fire broke out in the attic. It burned the four story wooden structure to the ground. This was especially unfortunate, as the brothers had only recently lowered the fire insurance from $100,000 to $75,000, apparently without consulting the "Power." Plans for a new family mansion, "one built to withstand anything," were soon formulated, resulting in the Hayes Mansion which we know today.

Mary, a religious pamphleteer, had gathered quite a flock of followers, and in 1903, founded her own Church of the True Life. Meeting in Edenvale and at the Unitarian Church on North Third Street, the congregations heard Mary preach sermons which were published the following week in the family's newspaper. Fire destroyed the Edenvale chapel in the same year that the church was formed.

Preaching, healing, and building a gigantic new mansion were too much for even Mary Hayes-Chynoweth. On July 27, 1905, at the age of eighty, she died peacefully in her new home, surrounded by her family and friends. Her last words were as if to answer an unasked question: *I have never wronged anyone.* It is said that Mary's spirit still makes its presence known on the Hayes estate.

Hayes Home Eden Vale, near San Jose, Cal.

*The "new" Hayes Mansion. Postcard courtesy of Jack Douglas.*

*James Duval Phelan*
*Courtesy of Bancroft Library.*

# Our Phelan Legacy

THERE MAY BE NO SINGLE INDIVIDUAL WHO HAS HAD the lasting impact on our valley's cultural life as did James Duval Phelan. This three-term mayor of San Francisco (1897-1901) and U.S. Senator (1915-1921) is remembered now for his Montalvo estate in the hills above Saratoga, however, a closer look at the record shows that Phelan and his family's association with San Jose and the valley go much farther back than the Montalvo period.

James D. Phelan, a native son, was born April 20, 1861 in San Francisco. His father, James Phelan Sr., came west during the gold rush, but he was more interested in mining gold from the prospectors than from the gold fields. The elder Phelan transferred merchandise from his store in the east to San Francisco just in time to supply the needs of the throngs who came for gold. He did so well that he was soon buying real estate and founding banks in San Francisco, San Jose and Santa Cruz. By the time young James had finished college at St. Ignatius College (now the University of San Francisco), his father owned a half dozen three-story office blocks in downtown San Jose, including the Alice Building on South Second, the Louise Building on Second and

San Fernando, the Martin block on North First, the New York Exchange block on North First, the Phelan block at Post and First and the Rucker Building on North Fourth. The family also had land holdings adjacent to what is now Phelan Avenue in south San Jose.

Young James had the temperament and inclination to become a poet, but the demands of the family business were to prevail. He did have time, however, to do the European tour and attend Hastings Law School before being put to work. Upon his father's death in 1892 he gained control of the family's vast fortune. His two sisters were also beneficiaries. Unlike his father, who lived for his business, the son used the family fortune to launch projects more to his fancy.

About this same time Phelan was named vice president of the California Commission to the World's Columbian Exhibition in Chicago (1893). It was at this great fair that the California Building, with its mission revival architecture and emphasis on western art, created such a sensation. Phelan made lasting friends of architect A. Page Brown and western artists such as William Keith. Brown would become a major figure in the rise of the pre-earthquake San Francisco cityscape. When San Jose businessmen

*Residence of Senator J.D. Phelan, Saratoga, California*

gathered to create the exclusive Sainte Claire Club, Phelan offered to build it for them, and he chose Brown to be the architect. Upon completion, Phelan donated the large California landscape by Keith which still hangs in the club lounge.

Phelan's first public office was the presidency of the San Francisco Art Association. One of his speeches on corruption in San Francisco politics convinced Fremont Older, crusading editor of the *San Francisco Bulletin*, to persuade Phelan to run for mayor.

Phelan did not forget San Jose during his years as mayor, for it was in 1898-99 that he conceived and created San Jose's first genuine opera house on North First Street. He named it the Victory Theatre in honor of the victories of the Spanish American War. The theatre opened with a performance of Sheridan's 18th century classic "A School for Scandal." During an intermission Phelan was coaxed upon the stage to say a few words: *Ladies and gentlemen, I cannot pardon Mr. Warde his treachery to his art in introducing me, a nineteenth century product in the midst of an antique play...there are among this large and elegant audience many of us to whom the drama is at once an amusement and a means of education..How long a time would it require an average man to acquire a sufficient fund of education in the manners, customs and habiliments of the times of which this play treats, are as easily and delightfully presented to us this evening?...Your kindness shall influence me in endeavoring to condone the fault of Mr. Warde in introducing me, a glaring anachronism, into his art.*

The Victory Theatre continued to be a principle venue for live entertainment for 50 years. It was destroyed by fire in the mid-60s.

Ex-mayor Phelan felt the full brunt of the earthquake and fire of 1906, both financially and emotionally. He lost most of his rare and autographed volumes as well as his own literary efforts, but it is characteristic that he demonstrated his concern for the plight of San Francisco by chairing the administration of relief and Red Cross funds.

Phelan played a large role in the restoration of

*Stained glass window depicts the 1542 voyage of
Juan Rodriguez Cabrillo who explored the Pacific coast.*

San Francisco. A supporter of a master plan by architect Daniel Burnham, Phelan was disappointed when the architect's "city beautiful" conception was only partially carried out. Perhaps it was this frustration that made Phelan decide to build his dream villa on the mountain in Santa Clara County.

Once again he returned to his experience with the California Building by choosing an architectural style that was compatible with the Spanish and early California influence. The excellent design of the spaces surrounding the home take advantage of the views and temperate climate. On every side there are terraces, patios and colonnaded walkways. So also

does the name reflect back to the 16th century Spanish writer Montalvo who first used the term California in a work of fiction.

Phelan was elected to the U.S. Senate in 1915 and was a supporter of Wilson's policies during World War I. Defeated in his attempt at a second term, and refusing offers of an ambassadorship, he went on a two-year world tour which resulted in a book about his experiences in various countries.

Subsequently he returned to Montalvo where he proceeded to entertain a veritable parade of literary and artistic types, many of whom he had known during his days as president of San Francisco's

Bohemian Club in the early 90s. He kept a suite available for California writer Gertrude Atherton who frequently retreated to Montalvo to write her popular novels of the "new woman" and life in pre-earthquake San Francisco.

Senator Phelan became associated with San Jose State through his friendship with poets Edwin Markham and Professor Henry Meade Bland. Dr. Bland's English Club members were annual guests at Montalvo for poetry readings, and they formed the nucleus of the Edwin Markham Poetry Society. The Senator attended the dedication of Markham's home (near the SJS campus) as a literary shrine and head-quarters for the Markham Society. (This house is now on the San Jose Historical Museum grounds.)

After a brief illness, the Senator died at his beloved Montalvo on August 7, 1930. In his lengthy will he provided for his many friends and associates, including endowments for Phelan and Markham Society literary awards, but must importantly, he deeded Montalvo to be a center for the arts. With its many programs such as the artist in residence pro-gram, its art shows, plays and musical performances, it has been a continual source of artistic renewal since its founding. The house and gardens remain an inspiration to all who visit there.

## The Phelan Library Project

With the pace of the many activities at the Villa it is difficult to get a real feeling for what the estate was like when the Senator lived there. With this in mind, the Phelan Library Committee was formed in 1986 to restore the Senator's library to its original state. Some of the Senator's original books and copies of titles that he is known to have owned fill the book cases, along with letters from and photographs of the many prominent artists, writers and statesmen who were frequent guests at Montalvo.

# Jackson Hatch:
# The Rise and Fall of a Public Man

W E ARE ALL DIMINISHED WHEN A PUBLIC FIGURE falls from grace, particularly one who represents the profession of law, the cornerstone of which, should be trust. For Jackson Hatch, twice his party's candidate for the State Supreme Court, an error of judgement resulted in a personal tragedy of almost Biblical proportions.

Jackson Hatch was a native son born in Tuolumne County on December 27, 1852. His father, F.L. Hatch, was a respected Superior Court judge of Colusa County. Jackson was educated in country schools, then began to make his living as a teacher while, at the same time, studying law. He was admitted to the California bar at the age of 21 and shortly after was elected District Attorney of Colusa County. He served in this position until 1880 when he went into private practice specializing in criminal law. In 1888 he was chosen first assistant U.S. Attorney in San Francisco.

Two years later he set up practice in San Jose in the old Porter Building at Second and Santa Clara Streets. Active in the Democratic Party and leader in

*From* Men of California. *Courtesy of San Jose State University Library Special Collections.*

the Elks and other organizations, he frequently was called upon to make public speeches as he did at the opening of our Carnegie Library in 1903. He was the Democratic candidate for the State Supreme Court in 1890 and again in 1906, and there was talk of his being the Democratic candidate for Governor. Though never a judge, he was referred to as Judge Hatch which was, at that time, a sign of respect given to prominent lawyers.

Hatch married in 1879 and had four children — three sons and a daughter. Sons Frank and George became lawyers in San Francisco. The family had a home on Alum Rock Avenue, then an area that was part of the county. When the rowdiness of the Alum Rock saloons became too much for the decent folks, Jackson Hatch was one of the people instrumental in incorporating the area into the City of East San Jose. The offending saloons were promptly closed. Hatch served as the city attorney and was personally responsible for getting the Carnegie Trust to fund the construction of the library at the corner of Santa Clara and 23rd Streets.

The 1906 campaign, the expenses of keeping up a high public profile and a serious eye operation apparently led to a need for additional income. It was at this time that he "borrowed" from a client's trust account. On January 11, 1908 Louis Sage, son of an elderly widow who had been Hatch's client since 1900, brought charges against the attorney for the embezzlement of $45,000.

Newspapers published rumors that Hatch had fled to Honduras or had attempted suicide. Although such thoughts may have crossed his mind, Hatch had too much character for such actions. Grand Jury hearings were held and there was no shortage of loyal Hatch supporters there, including the rector of Trinity Church and other leading attorneys such as Louis Oneal, Frank Freeman and Owen D. Richardson, all of whom represented the defendant at the first trial.

In his defense Hatch stated that Mrs. Sage had approved his borrowing funds from her trust fund, and that as executor he had complete control over use of the funds. There was no evidence that he had attempted to hide his transactions, and it seemed that much of the amount in question had been expended properly in her behalf. There was evidence, however, that Hatch had forged Mrs. Sage's name on some papers. Hatch could raise only $5,000 to repay his client, but the payment was refused in order to "see that justice be done."

Arthur M. Free, District Attorney, led the prosecution and Judge J.R. Welch presided over the trial. On December 25, 1910 Jackson Hatch was convicted of embezzlement of $37,000 and sentenced to 5 years in San Quentin. On appeal the verdict was reversed and a second trial was held. Welch chose to again be presiding judge in spite of protests from Hatch's attorneys that the judge was prejudiced against their client.

This prejudice became more apparent as the process ground forward. Unlike the first trial when the defendant was free on bail, Welch had Hatch incarcerated in the county jail. When Hatch was convicted again, this time for embezzlement of $4,100, Welch increased the sentence from 5 to 7 years.

Once again an appeals court, on a vote of 2 to 1, reversed the decision, but the case was appealed to the Supreme Court where the conviction was upheld by a single vote. Welch denied probation even though the defendant had already spent 2 years in the county jail.

Hatch's time in the county jail had been ameliorated somewhat by the sheriff's kindness in allowing the cell to be furnished with personal belongings and by giving Mrs. Hatch permission to come and go freely and sometimes remain in the cell during the day. But after 4 years of trials and bouts of recurrent blindness, the 60 year old attorney had to face the ultimate humiliation of being sent to San Quentin.

Considering his condition, it seemed unlikely that Hatch would ever leave San Quentin alive, but after 2 years of appeals to the prison board and the governor, he was paroled. He and his wife moved to Oakland where they began a campaign to get clemency and a pardon from the Governor so that Hatch could again practice law. Hatch's file in the state archive is full of letters from judges, attorneys, clergymen, congressmen and other officials to Governor Hiram Johnson. Even District Attorney Free and Judge Welch wrote that they would have no objections to a pardon. Only the Santa Clara Bar Association, which thought that a pardon would sidetrack their efforts to have Hatch disbarred, wrote objections.

The pardon was granted in December 1918 and after 2 more years of bureaucratic maneuvers Jackson Hatch was allowed to practice law again in partnership with his sons in San Francisco. Freedom and the ability to again earn a living must have been only slight consolation to this now elderly and broken man. He died in 1924 without so much as a notice in the newspaper of the city where he had once been a leading citizen.

*Prison mug shots courtesy of California State Archives.*

# Dr. Howard B. Gates & His Maybeck House

DR. HOWARD B. GATES IS REMEMBERED TODAY primarily for his home at 625 South Thirteenth Street which was designed by the noted architect Bernard Maybeck. Son of a pioneer educator, Howard rose to become one of the most respected medical men in the county.

Howard Gates was born in 1867 in the San Jose Institute, a private school run by his father Freeman. As a boy, young Howard probably rode the first horse cars out The Alameda all the way to downtown Santa Clara, fished in Guadalupe Creek, and marveled at the new-fangled electric lighting on the 230 foot tower sitting astride the intersection of Market and Santa Clara Streets. Being the son of a schoolmaster, he no doubt had less time for play than other boys.

Gates attended U.C. Berkeley during the period when Bernard Maybeck was commissioned by Phoebe Hearst to make a master plan for that campus. It is possible that he may have met the great architect at this time; at any rate he would have been aware of Maybeck's work.

After graduating from Berkeley, Gates enrolled in Cooper Medical College in San Francisco. He later received his MD degree from New York's Homeopathic College.

Dr. Gates returned to San Jose in 1895 and began his practice in the old Porter Building at Second and Santa Clara Streets. Two years later he married Amelia Levenson, also an MD, and they soon had a thriving practice at their Gates Sanitarium at Eleventh and Santa Clara. This location, then on the edge of town, would later attract other medical establishments, including San Jose Hospital.

By 1904 the Gates' were affluent enough to have their custom built home erected on Thirteenth Street, just two blocks from their sanitarium. Howard's hope of walking to work was short lived, however, as he was soon to be appointed superintendent of the County Hospital, and this would require that he take the "Big Red" streetcars across town.

The earthquake of '06 caused extensive damage to many local buildings. St. Patrick's Church on Santa Clara, the Normal School on Washington Square, and the County Hospital were left in total ruin. It became Dr. Gates' greatest challenge to supervise the reconstruction of the County Hospital.

Howard and Amelia took a two year sabbatical in 1908 and traveled to Berlin, Vienna and Zurich to brush up on the latest surgical techniques.

Although hardly 40, Howard's heavy workload

*Gates-Maybeck House, 62 S. 13th Street. Photo by Dennis Skaggs.*

was taking its toll on his health, and in 1909, his family convinced him to relocate to the Los Angeles area. Soon after, he suffered a serious mental breakdown. In 1913 he recrossed the Atlantic to take the cure in Sorrento on the Bay of Naples. His condition worsened and he was moved to Rome where he lived out his last days surrounded by his family which now included an adopted son.

*Howard B. Gates, 1867-1914. Photo from* Reminiscences of Santa Clara Valley and San Jose, California *by A. Mars.*

The end came on May 1, 1914, just a few months before the continent was swept up in the "Great War." The cause of his tragic death at age 47 was diagnosed as an acute case of "peripheral neuritis." One can't help wondering if that 2 year trip abroad in 1908-09 had not been a fruitless search to find a cure for this mental illness. Perhaps he consulted with Freud while in Vienna.

Gates' body was cremated in Rome and returned to California. The records at Oak Hill Cemetery indicate that his ashes were buried there when his mother was interred in the family plot in 1920. There is no inscription on the stone, however, so he lies in an unmarked grave in the section of Oak Hill which is reserved for San Jose pioneers.

Gates' singular Maybeck home remains a monument to this unique individual whose life began in frontier San Jose and ended so tragically in the eternal city of Rome. The house is the only structure in San Jose designed by the California architect Bernard Maybeck (1862-1957).

Bernard Maybeck, son of an immigrant wood-carver, was sent by his father to Paris in 1881 to learn furniture design. While in Paris, he decided to follow his true bent and enrolled in the famous Ecole des Beaux-Arts which was the seat of classicism in the arts. Maybeck's classical training would serve him time and again, when as an architect in San Francisco, he combined a myriad of classical styles into romantic dream houses which his skeptical peers labeled "creative eclecticism."

Using local materials, especially redwood, and extensive landscaping, Maybeck and others created California's first original architecture, referred to as the San Francisco Bay Tradition. Maybeck's two most outstanding landmarks in the Bay area are the Palace of Fine Arts, created for the Pan Pacific Exposition of 1914, and the Christian Science Church in Berkeley. The architect's less imposing, but in many ways more fascinating creations, were the many private homes he designed around the Bay Area. The greatest accumulation of these fanciful homes is in the hills on the north side of the Berkeley campus where Maybeck himself lived.

The Maybeck homes are adapted to northern California living, i.e., they conform to our regional climatic conditions, and they extend the free flow of space by eliminating the distinction between indoors and out of doors. His hill houses make extensive use of balconies, rooms which open onto gardens, and large cathedral height windows which make the rooms seem more spacious then they actually are. The lavish use of carved redwood on the interiors and exteriors, and the delicate gothic tracery windows were all evidence that Maybeck didn't stray too far from his father's profession. Maybeck believed, as did his internationally famous contemporary, Frank Lloyd Wright, that the home should blend in with the natural landscape that surround it.

Much of Maybeck's domestic work prior to the earthquake reflected his interest in Swiss, German and English medieval styles. The house he designed for Howard B. Gates in San Jose is a good example of his eclectic genius. Basically Italian in design, its extended roof line, forming a cover for elaborately sculptured baroque balconies, gives the upper portion of the house a Swiss flavor. What appears from the street to be a home of one and one half stories, is actually three stories high. The first story, lowered into the grade, includes the kitchen and dining room and servant's room. A large oval shaped opening in the rear leads from the dining area onto what was a sunken garden. A circular stair leads from the lowered first floor to the spacious living room and on up to the bedrooms which are tucked neatly into what one would normally consider the attic space. Natural light comes in from the numerous rear windows and skylights.

Perhaps the eventual restoration of this elegant house will include an outside finish of the original darker earthen hue and the extensive landscaping that characterized most of Maybeck's distinctive designs.

# Albert Solon: Master Tile Artist

*Albert Solon's photo from 1918 San Jose State Normal School Yearbook.*

WITH THE WANING OF THE INTERNATIONAL SCHOOL of Architecture and their bland colorless glass boxes, architects are considering the use of decoration on their "post modern" structures. This, of course, is nothing new, as most of our buildings from the 1880s to the ornate deco buildings of the 1920s and 30s were lavishly covered with terra cotta or glazed ceramic tile. Resistant to sun and weather, terra cotta could be molded into any desired shape or design.

Most of our older buildings in downtown San Jose are covered with terra cotta surfaces. The firm of Gladding and McBean, with its principal plant at Lincoln in Placer County, molded and fired the terra cotta siding for most of San Jose's early buildings as well as major structures throughout the west.

Some of our best examples are the St. James Post Office, the Twohy and Dohrman buildings, the Sainte Claire Building and the Sainte Claire Hotel. The old Bank of America and the Medico Dental use terra cotta in their decorative elements.

Besides architectural terra cotta, brightly colored ceramic tile was frequently used for decorative purposes on California buildings as far back as the Mission period. Modern use began at the turn of the century with the craftsman and Spanish revival movements in architectural design. San Jose became the west coast center for decorative tiles when Albert Solon and Frank Schemmel set up their S & S tile studio and plant in 1920.

Solon, who was born at Stoke-on-Trent in Staffordshire, England, was descended from a family which had been in the pottery and ceramic industry for 300 years. The Solon clan began perfecting their craft near Toulouse, France in 1680, and they eventually became recognized masters throughout Europe. Moving to England during the French Revolution, the family continued work at the famous Mintons factory. Solon's father, an author/expert on English china, perfected the process of painting with white clay on a black body, a technique which won him the highest awards at the Paris Exposition in 1878.

Young Albert, after serving his apprenticeship in England, came to San Jose in 1916 to teach ceramics at the San Jose Normal School. The practical arts were an essential part of teacher training, and one of the courses he taught was Rural School Pottery in which teachers learned to make clay objects from local materials and improvised firing methods. He taught physics when he wasn't busy in the pottery studio.

Solon left San Jose Normal and began his business in 1920. Applying methods used for making fine

*Old Home Economics Building at San Jose State University. Photo courtesy of Jack Douglas.*

---

china, Solon created ceramic tile masterpieces. His fine glazes gave the tiles a luminosity and transparency which made treasures of the buildings they decorated. Used for floors, stairs, fountains, wall treatments, fireplaces, mantles and archways, the tile set off the otherwise monochromatic character of a Spanish colonial revival home or courtyard. Good examples are the El Paseo court at 42 South First Street and the former Cambiano Art Fixtures shop at 798 South Second Street. Both of these buildings have courtyards with ornate tile fountains as well as other features.

Solon's art is brilliantly displayed on the old Home Economics Building at San Jose State which was built in 1921 and the Science Building (1931). Many of the Spanish Revival school buildings designed by William Weeks feature Solon's decorative touch, including the old Campbell High School.

As their reputation spread, the firm of Solon and Schemmel had to move from their quarters at Fourth and Carrie streets to a larger plant at 1881 South First, and Frank Schemmel, who handled the business end, moved his offices to the Monadnock Building in San Francisco.

During the building boom of the late 1920s, Solon's tile work was used on many major San Francisco landmarks including the Mark Hopkins Hotel, the Steinhart Aquarium and the ornate Don Lee auto show rooms. Perhaps the most noted building to utilize Solon tile is the Hearst Castle at San Simeon. (Solon's brother Camille was an assistant to Julia Morgan, Hearst's architect.)

Solon returned to the making of china in 1932

when he joined with George J. Poxon in the manufacture of a new style of almost indestructible dinnerware called Sainte Claire china. Poxon, who had been a fellow apprentice with Solon in England, discovered a Death Valley mineral that was ideal for such china. (Gladding and McBean later came out with a similar product popularly known as Franciscan Ware.)

When Schemmel retired from the business in 1937, Paul G. Larkin became Solon's partner. Larkin, who had learned the business by working at Garden City Pottery, would eventually take over the business in 1947.

Albert Solon and his wife Emma raised three children in their South 16th Street home. He was active in the Elks, was president of the San Jose Lion's Club, and kept up his relationship with San Jose State through the Alumni Association. He died suddenly of a heart attack on August 2, 1949 while visiting his daughter in Santa Barbara. In addition to his brother Camille, there were also Philip who made fine porcelain in New Jersey, and Leon, a world authority on architectural polychrome and a celebrated muralist, portrait painter and ceramist. It is not known how many of the Solon offspring entered the ceramics field, but it would be a pity if 300 years of tradition had died out after only one generation in the new world.

Albert Solon is remembered by very few, but there is probably no architect or artist whose work may be seen in so many places, from modest suburban homes to hotels and monuments such as San Simeon. Many buildings which displayed his art have been torn down or carelessly remodeled.

Only recently, with the rise of the preservation movement, have many of the architectural details of our older buildings been noted and appreciated. Once one becomes aware of these colorful ceramic gems, they seem to shine out everywhere. Solon and his ancient art continues to brighten our lives.

*Courtyard of the Sainte Claire Hotel, 1926. Tile work by Solon and Schemmel of San Jose. San Jose State University Archives.*

# Carol Henning: The Girl From The Class of '24

HENNING, CAROL "Husky"
Ambition — To be a Ph.D.
Hobby — Taking nourishment.
Characteristic — Ambition.

*From* The Bell, *1924, Yearbook of San Jose High School, San Jose State University Library Special Collections.*

BUDDING AUTHOR JOHN STEINBECK MAY NOT HAVE gone looking for a woman who could be supportive and yet critical, tough minded yet good humored, and satisfied to live in near poverty with a man who was reclusive and almost totally absorbed in his art, but he met her, not in the literary set at Stanford or in the tough New York newspaper world, but in a fish hatchery at Lake Tahoe.

Carol Henning, the woman who became his alter ego and helpmate during the years of struggle and eventual success, was born in San Jose and raised in a house near the San Jose State campus. The two met by chance when Carol and her sister Idell dropped in on the Tahoe City fish hatchery where John was working during the summer of 1928.

John was bowled over by Carol's forthright manner, wit and down-to-earth skepticism. In a letter written to a friend prior to their marriage he said: *I'd like you to know Carol. She doesn't write or dance or play the piano and she has very little of any soul at all. But horses like her and dogs and little boys and boot blacks and laborers. But people with souls don't like her much.* (Benson biography, p.161)

Though solidly middle class, Carol was equally at home with working people and the Cannery Row crowd who hung around Ed Ricketts' lab. After their marriage in 1930, Carol pretty much supported John until his first real success, *Of Mice and Men*, was published in 1937. During those lean years Carol typed all of John's handwritten manuscripts and was his most reliable critic. It was she who suggested the titles for *Of Mice and Men* and *Grapes of Wrath*. The latter he dedicated: *to Carol who willed this book.*

The success of these two books thrust the author upon the public stage. Carol's role as buffer between the writer and the world dissolved, and the important function of critic was taken over by his agent Elizabeth Otis. After the memorable voyage to the Gulf of California with Ed Ricketts and the crew of the Western Flyer, Carol and John were separated and then divorced in 1943. The end of their relationship also signaled the end of what was perhaps the most significant period of the author's career.

In an attempt to help the war effort and forget John, Carol enrolled in a mechanics course at Fort Ord and graduated at the head of the class. After the war she became a career public information officer for the Red Cross in Carmel. During that period she married William Brown, a prominent Monterey resident. They lived in Carmel until her death in 1983.

In order to discover more about Carol prior to her meeting with John, I have done some research into her life in San Jose. Carol was the eldest of two daughters of Wilbur and Nellie Henning. Wilbur Henning rose to be vice president of a leading real estate and investment firm and was active in community affairs. The family lived in a comfortable home they had built in the then fashionable Naglee Park neighborhood. Carol and her sister Idell were only a year apart in school and were apparently very close. They attended San Jose High School when it shared a Washington Square location with San Jose State College.

The rare photo of Carol as a young woman, which is reproduced here, is from the high school yearbook of 1924. Many of the traits to which Steinbeck was attracted seem to be reflected there. The apparently self-applied captions were not meant

Carol and John Steinbeck in the early 1930s. John Steinbeck Research Center, San Jose State University.

to be serious, but they are interesting in retrospect. Perhaps a reflection of her independent nature or maturity is the fact that she was not listed among the members of any club or organization.

A further indication of such qualities was her departure after graduation for San Francisco. She first worked as an executive assistant at the August Schilling Co., then later, at the time she met Steinbeck, she was working as an advertising assistant at the *San Francisco Chronicle*.

Although they didn't know her well, classmates such as Ernest Renzel, Theron Fox and Vivian Chubb whom I interviewed all remembered her with respect, and none were surprised that she had married a famous writer.

Some might consider it an act of fate that she met and fell in love with the aspiring young novelist. What would his work have been like without her? And what might he have written if circumstances had allowed them to remain together?

House that John and Carol Steinbeck built in the mountains above Los Gatos in 1939. John completed the manuscript for Grapes of Wrath here. Photo from the Steinbeck Research Center, San Jose State University.

# Cora Older: Of Romance and Roses

*Cora Baggerly Older in the 1890s. Courtesy of Bancroft Library.*

FOR TWO GENERATIONS CORA BAGGERLY OLDER WAS the literary lioness of Santa Clara County. She was one of the regulars at Senator Phelan's Montalvo literary soirees and also of the San Francisco writer's groups. Her influence on the arts in this area runs deep. Cora's life after she and her husband settled into their country home in the hills above Cupertino in 1913 could be symbolized by romance and roses.

Cora was born in Clyde, New York on October 24, 1874, and she first came to California on a visit in 1892. It was at a play in Sacramento that she first met Fremont Older who was a reporter on the local paper. It was not long before they were married, and he began his career as the crusading editor of the *San Francisco Bulletin.*

Those turbulent times when Older and Rudolph Spreckles stood almost alone against a thoroughly corrupt city government were reflected in Cora's writing of that period. Her social realist novels included: *The Socialist and the Prince* (1903); *The*

*Giants* (1904); and *Esther Damon* (1911). Her numerous articles and reviews appeared in journals and in the *Bulletin.*

All of this changed for Cora when the Olders built "Woodhills," their country home. In this idyllic setting Cora became increasingly fascinated by the romance of early California. In this she had much in common with her old San Francisco friend James Phelan who had recently built Villa Montalvo just a few miles away. Life in and around the California missions during the Spanish period would be a primary subject of Cora's writings to follow.

Fremont and Cora were early automobile enthusiasts, and on one of their trips in 1908, their car broke down in the vicinity of San Juan Bautista. While waiting to get repairs, they became acquainted with the local priest, Father Closa. In their conversation the Olders suggested that the local citizens put on a fiesta to raise funds for the mission. The fiesta, which ran for two days and included a rodeo, was a great success and netted $4,000 for the restoration of the mission.

Once established at Woodhills, Cora began researching the early history of San Jose and Santa Clara County. On September 19, 1916 she began a series of articles under the heading "When San Jose Was Young," which appeared almost daily in the *San Jose News.* Her name never appeared on any of these pieces which were prefaced by the statement: *A series of interesting articles of an historical nature prepared especially for the News by a well-known author and journalist.* It has never been made clear if Cora chose anonymity because her name was associated with a rival Bay Area newspaper (the *Bulletin*) or because

*Fiesta de las Rosas. San Jose Historical Museum Collections.*

her brother Hiland "Hi" Baggerly was managing editor of the *News*.

Cora had the perspicacity to understand that there were still people living in the area who could remember San Jose from the Mexican period, and her diaries of that period document the excitement she had in locating them and getting their stories. Her novelist's eye would seek out the romance in the simple lives of the early Californians. She tracked down and interviewed relatives of the bandit Tiburcio Vasquez, as well as survivors of the Donner Party. She wrote numerous stories about the native Indians. In one of these she wrote: *One of the race tragedies is the disappearance of the California Indian under the Spanish and American conquests. Occasional hunters meet a survivor of the old tribes living alone in the mountains, but for the most part the Indians about San Jose are a shadow people.* She would return to these subjects years later in her popular books: *California Missions and their Romances (1938)* and *Love Stories of Old California* (1940).

An early preservationist, Cora saved one of San Jose's original adobe buildings which stood near West Santa Clara Street. She had it moved to Woodhills and reconstructed it as a rustic study near their swimming pool. Around it she planted roses in the fashion of a mission garden, and she asked her friends to donate one distinctive decorative tile (she called them "memory tiles") to be placed in the walks and walls of the garden. These tiles are still a unique aspect of the garden.

She was a guiding force in the production of the Fiesta de las Rosas festivals which began in 1926. Perhaps an outgrowth of her experience years before at San Juan Bautista, the Fiesta was an elaborate four day affair of plays, pageants, dances and a rose parade which rivaled Pasadena's. One of Cora's fiesta projects was a Shakespeare garden — an exhibit that included all of the flowers mentioned in the works of the Bard. Each festival featured an original play based upon an early California theme. These were produced by the students, faculty, staff and families of San Jose State and were staged under the stars using the Spanish Revival campus buildings as a backdrop. Cora's play, *The Madonna of Monterey*, was the hit of the 1930 season. The fiestas continued to be held annually until 1933 when they met their end as a result of the depression.

Cora Older's enthusiasm for local history led her to suggest to Senator Phelan that he offer the Sainte Claire Club building to the county for a museum. Phelan had constructed the building for the club but had kept ownership. Cora had many plans for the museum, including a permanent Shakespeare garden at the rear of the building. Phelan even agreed to donate $5,000 for conversion. Cora, however, was up against some hard headed members of the Board of Supervisors who wanted the building for a county library instead. Even though the building was free and came with $5,000, they refused to accept the offer because they didn't want the long-term expense of maintaining it. The Sainte Claire Club members must have sighed with relief when they purchased the building a short time later.

In 1927 Cora Older and Mrs. Charles Derby convinced the city council to set aside a 5 1/2 acre tract of land at Naglee and Dana Avenues for a municipal rose garden. Expert advice was solicited from the great San Francisco landscape architect John McLaren, and funds were supplied by the Santa Clara Rose Society. Cora's unique and appropriate contribution was a collection of old mission roses from all but three of the 21 California mission gardens.

*Cora and Fremont Older.*

In 1918 William Randolph Hearst wooed Fremont Older away from the *Bulletin* to become managing editor of his *San Francisco Call* (later to be renamed the *Call Bulletin* when Hearst acquired the latter). Cora and her husband collaborated on a biography of Hearst's father Senator George Hearst. Cora followed in 1936 with a biography of William Randolph.

Fremont Older died in 1935 and was buried at Woodhills in the same plot with his favorite dogs. Cora lived on at her beloved home, continuing the tradition of Sunday dinners with important people of the day. Ex-convicts were often among the guests (one of Fremont's crusades had been for prison reform). A number of Cora's garden staff were former inmates.

Cora kept busy writing and officiating at numerous local PEN writers conferences and events. Her last book: *San Francisco: A Magic City* was published when she was in her mid-80's. Carl Sandburg called it "one of the best books done about an American city." She was working on a book which would have included a romance story from every state in the union when she died on September 26, 1968, age 93.

One of the Older's lasting monuments was their home at Woodhills. The house was allowed to slip into almost complete ruin until purchased by the Mid-peninsula Open Space District. Former newspaper publisher Mort Levine and his wife Elaine have leased the home from the district and lovingly restored it to its original glory. They maintain it as their home and as a showplace for those interested in the Olders and their time there. Occasional tours are offered to the public through the Open Space District.

Fremont Older occupies a distinguished place in the pantheon of American newspapermen. Cora, whose literary output (except for *California Missions*) is pretty much forgotten, should be remembered for the many cultural contributions she made to San Jose and environs. The next time you visit our Municipal Rose Garden remember Cora Older. The romance may be fading, but the roses live on.

## Cora Older Meets The Great Morosco

This is the story of the production, in 1929, of Cora Older's play, *Someone in White*, by the legendary Broadway producer Oliver Morosco.

Unfortunately for those concerned, the drama of producing the play was probably more engrossing than Mrs. Older's playscript. The cast of characters in this real drama included: Cora Older, successful novelist, journalist and historian; Fremont Older, crusading San Francisco newspaper editor and Cora's husband; Oliver Morosco, a Broadway producer who began his career at 16 managing the old Auditorium Theatre in San Jose; James D. Phelan, patron of the arts; Helen McRuer, stagestruck young actress; and Jack Black, ex-convict and prison reformer.

Morosco had made millions producing a run of successful plays on Broadway, including such classics as: *Abie's Irish Rose, Peg O' My Heart, So Long Letty, Canary Cottage,* and *Bird of Paradise,* but he had lost it all to former wives and unfortunate business ventures. In the depths of alcoholic despair the great man had found new hope when the enthusiastic would-be actress Helen McRuer took over his life. Their new venture was a drama school in San Francisco's old Aladdin Studio. Not satisfied, however, with just training actors, Morosco was soon scouting about for successful plays and backers. The plays turned out to be Cora's, but the backers were more elusive.

Cora Older and Oliver Morosco must have looked forward to their partnership with high expectations — Cora to the expert play handling that Morosco could provide, plus the magic of his name, and Morosco to a good play by an experienced writer, especially one with influential friends who could come up with financial backing.

Enter Senator James D. Phelan. In 1911 Phelan had invested in Richard Walton Tully's play *The Bird of Paradise* which, with Morosco's artful adaptation, became one of Broadway's longest running plays. Morosco, who must have been aware of Phelan's long friendship with the Olders, no doubt assumed that Phelan's support would be forthcoming for any Cora Older play. In March 1928 he tried to interest the Senator in Mrs. Older's play about early California: *Madonna of Monterey.* Phelan replied: *I regret I am not interested in the production. I have lost faith in the legitimate stage... .*

Undaunted, the producer appealed again for

Oliver Morosco from The Oracle of Broadway.

*Someone in White* in a letter dated January 6, 1929: *My Dear Mr. Phelan, While I realize that you did not fare very well with Mr. Tully's last play, of which I had nothing to do with and while I further realize that dappling into this profession is not necessary for you to do, I want at least to tell you what I have that I feel will make us much, if not more money than the Bird. It is a play written by Mrs. Fremont Older and I have been working on it for a long time, just as I did the revision of the Bird.*

*It has two acts, the utmost comedy values, a serious moral story and in the end it teaches a lesson not be be forgotten. It further has "money value" of being laid in a house of prostitution, which is legalized in Nevada where the action of the first two acts takes place. The third act is in Santa Clara County where the prostitutes under proper guidance have turned respectable. It has drama, comedy, atmosphere, tears, scenic effects, lighting effects of a novel nature and is not "slushy" or common in any sense of the word.*

*It is a beautifully written play, 12 characters, 2 settings. I have assured Mrs. Older a production of this play and she deferred a trip to Europe in order to see her brainchild developed. With its comparatively small cast and only two settings the production expense will not be great and it is my idea to present it in San Francisco first, then up and down the Coast where I am egotistical enough to believe my name will help a great deal. Then it is my thought to take the play to New York in September, get a run out of it there. It if goes over big there, I can mount eight companies throughout the U.S. and Canada the year following.*

*Since my smash (bankruptcy) in New York, where*

*I was robbed of all my possessions, I had a setback which I presume is natural but my old fighting energy is regained itself and I feel more fit to do big things now than ever before. I lack the money to properly produce the play, although I can get some of it, but rather than a lot of associates I would prefer one, naturally that one is yourself. $7,500 will be sufficient and if you care to entertain the proposition this would entitle you to 37$\frac{1}{2}$%.*

*I would like to make a comeback Sir, because with you I had my first New York success and I believe history can repeat itself... .*

Morosco's plea fell on deaf ears, and when Cora found out that he had gone to Phelan she was outraged. It was only when Morosco told her of his earlier dealings with the Senator that her feelings were assuaged. Attempts to get Fremont Older to invest were also fruitless. Cora's diary for May 20th reads: *Morosco did a stupid thing today of going to Fremont and asking him for $5,000. Fremont said he might try a Faro bank, but not that...the month of June was impossible for a play, a new play, especially in midsummer...and he'd have nothing to do with it.* Morosco was undeterred and proceeded with the production, hoping that an "angel" would eventually turn up.

Helen McRuer, who had put her girlhood idol on the comeback trail, was as surprised as anyone when, at a cast party, the great man proposed marriage (his third), the ceremony to take place in the fall when the play was into its New York run. Helen's faith in the play and Morosco was so great that she convinced her parents to mortgage their home to help finance it.

*Someone in White* had many characteristics of some of Cora's earlier stories. Though in a contemporary setting, it has a madonna-like character who comes into the lives of the outcast women and brings about miraculous changes. There are corrupt politicians and businessmen and also petty criminals who, if given a break, could become useful citizens. An ex-convict, Jack Black, who he had been saved from a lifetime in prison by Fremont Older, helped Cora on the dialogue for the underworld types.

Like all the playwrights Morosco had worked with, Cora had a difficult time accepting the Master's revisions. Her diary during the rehearsals is sprinkled with comments such as: *Most unhappy day of my life, Morosco scorned the suggestions and I lost my temper... It makes me furious that he goes around saying he puts lines into my play when he is as illiterate as a horse... If anyone killed a theatrical producer, I'd acquit him...*

*Morosco and his new bride bid farewell to San Francisco in 1929. Photo from* The Oracle of Broadway.

*Editors seem white knights in comparison with the theatrical people.*

Morosco assembled a credible cast for the play. Charlotte Walker played the miracle worker, Ari Lorenz Blanche the tough madam of the Nevada bawdy house, and Morosco's fiancee played the role of her daughter. The discoverer of such stars as Richard Dix, Charles Ruggles, Marjorie Rambeau, Charlotte Greenwood and Eddie Cantor felt his reputation so secure that on the marquee and the programs he listed only himself, the star and the phrase: *and a typical Morosco cast.*

The old Capitol Theatre at Market and Ellis Streets was chosen for the premiere. Cora hoped that the "popular" ticket prices (25 cents to $1) would draw the public down from the theater district near Union Square. The budget for advertising was woefully inadequate, but the playwright's reputation as a local celebrity led to a number of articles describing the play and the motivations behind it.

*Someone in White* opened on June 15, 1929. Cora wrote in her diary: *a good crowd, I knew many, but the balcony wasn't filled because it rained all day nearly. I think the play was liked though many were amazed by it. I made a speech after they had all come out (curtain call). I called Jack Black, who had arrived from New York just to surprise us the first night. Jack came up and bowed. I explained that Jack had helped me with the play.* Cora had invited Phelan to the opening, but the Senator, perhaps not wishing to confront Morosco, failed to appear.

The reviews the following day were not encouraging. Cora summed them up in her diary: The Examiner *critic was friendly, the* Chronicle *hostile and the* Mercury *nice, the* Bulletin *friendly, the* News *hostile and of course the* Post Enquirer's *Levant naturally unfriendly because he had been dismissed by Fremont...the* Argonaut *and the* Monitor *roasted it.* Cora managed to get Phelan to a performance and was downhearted when he criticized the religious aspects of the last act.

Morosco had launched the play with loans and promises, hoping that a successful opening would draw investors. These didn't materialize and after the first week the stagehands were threatening to strike if they weren't paid. More promises kept the play open until the 29th of June when a suit for back wages brought against the producer closed it.

To her credit, Cora seemed more concerned about Morosco's future than the failure of her play. On July 3rd she wrote: *Morosco looked terribly tattered and intoxicated. I don't think a thing can ever come of him again, he is down in the gutter.*

Cora pulled herself together and was soon back polishing up her play *Madonna of Monterey* for its premiere at the following spring's Fiesta de las Rosas. Senator Phelan died in August of that year (1930). Morosco gathered himself together enough to marry Helen McRuer in November and together they set off for Los Angeles and further adventures.

*Jose Theatre, built in 1904. Note Fatty Arbuckle in group on left, directly under Theatre Jose sign. San Jose Historical Museum Collections.*

# Downtown Movie Memories

O N MAY 18, 1984 CAMERA THREE BECAME THE first new theatre to open in downtown San Jose in 35 years. As Mayor Tom McEnery remarked at the dedication, it was good to see San Jose regain a little of its former reputation as a theatre town.

A brief look at the historical records affirms the Mayor's statement. When the last previous downtown theatre was opened (the Studio in 1950), there were six other movie houses operating on First Street, two on Second Street, and another on Market. For those who didn't want to come all the way down-town, there were the neighborhood theatres: the Garden on Lincoln Ave., the Mayfair on East Santa Clara, and the Towne on The Alameda.

As in other cities, San Jose's moving picture hous-es evolved from the local theatrical stage. Due to its strategic location on the main railroad line running along the coast, San Jose was on a major theatrical circuit and, according to Theron Fox, most of the traveling theatrical troupes played in San Jose prior to opening in San Francisco. At the turn of the century the first movies began to share the billing with the numerous live acts — a vibrant film era was beginning.

*Exterior of the Victory Theatre of San Jose. Photo taken from* Reminiscences of Santa Clara Valley and San Jose, California *by A. Mars.*

Sid Grauman, who later became the legendary Hollywood film mogul, got his start here in San Jose with the opening of his Unique Theatre on East Santa Clara in 1903. Although Grauman was to have theatres in several other northern California cities, it was here that he discovered Fatty Arbuckle who was working at a local restaurant as a singing waiter. Grauman immediately signed Fatty up as a performer at the Unique for $35 per week and one meal per day. Always the showman, Grauman arranged to have Fatty displayed in the front window of a local Greek restaurant so that the public could watch this new discovery engorge the equivalent of ten normal dinners. Al Jolson, another Grauman find, also began his long song and dance career on the stage of the Unique.

Perhaps San Jose's most venerable stage and film house was the Victory Theatre which was located on North First near the former Penney's store. The Victory, built by Senator James D. Phelan, opened its doors on February 2, 1899 with a production of Sheridan's *A School for Scandal*. Oliver Morosco, of San Francisco's "Morosco Grand Opera," ran theatricals in the Victory during the early years. In a single month in 1920 you could see such diverse entertainments as, David Belasco's *Daddies*, and Ibsen's *Ghosts*. By 1930, the Victory, now known as the Victory Vitaphone, was showing such films as *Love Among the Millionaires* with Clara Bow, *Near the Rainbow's End* with Bob Steele, and, *A Murder Case* with Laurel and Hardy. The Victory remained a mixed venue (offering some live theatre) right

through the Second World War. In the early fifties this grand old house was renamed the Crest Theatre and lived out its last years as a second run movie house. It was destroyed by fire in the mid-sixties.

Name changes were a common occurrence in the history of our local theatres. The Jose Theatre, built in 1904, is the only one of the older generation to have kept its original name.

For a little trip down memory lane, let's see how

*Fox Mission circa 1938. Courtesy of Steve Levin.*

many of you old-time movie buffs can remember these theatres as we move south on First Street from the Victory. At 32 North First we had the Lumina (1910-15) later called the Class A. A movie house called the Scenic operated briefly around 1910 at 119 South First. By 1913 it had reverted to retail as Bloom and Sons. James Beatty, San Jose's first movie theatre magnate, who owned the Jose on South Second, and the Liberty on South Market, had a theatre called the American at 141 South First. Beatty's American closed in 1925 when he sold all of his theatres to the National Theatre Syndicate. The Liberty Theatre was called the National for a number of years following the sale.

In 1933, The Padre Theatre opened at 145 South First. The Padre, later called the Fox Padre, was noted for westerns, and supplied a steady stream of oaters starring the likes of Randolph Scott and Johnny Mack Brown. The Padre was razed in the mid 60s. One of the most popular showplaces in town was the Theatre Deluxe which opened in 1913 at 230 South First. The name Theatre Deluxe was too much of a mouthful for San Jose moviegoers and it wasn't long before it was known as the "T & D." The T & D was later renamed the California, and even later the Fox California. (Things get complicated here.) At that point the Fox chain built their ultimate movie palace a block down the street which they christened the California Theatre. The old Fox California was renamed the Mission, later the Fox Mission.

Vying with the T & D for the customers' admissions was the Leowe's Hippodrome at 261 South First. There in 1920, you could catch a movie and a "super vaudeville show" for 30¢ for adults and a dime for kids. In a typical evening the customers might see such rousing silents as, *His Temporary Wife*, or *The Soul of Youth*, and on the same bill, the Hippodrome offered Pasquale and Powers—Magicians, Richard Walley and Co.—Jugglers, the Meryl Price Girl's Quartet, Dan McLean—Baritone, and Francis Owen and Co. doing a skit entitled: *Grandpa*. The Hippodrome later became the State Theatre, The American, and then finally the U A Theatre until it was demolished in the early 70s.

Local theatre history was made in April of 1927 with the grand opening of the California Theatre (now the Fox Theatre) at 345 South First Street. Designed by the firm of Weeks and Day, the California was San Jose's entry into the movie palace era. Built to seat 1700, this ornately decorated Spanish Baroque showplace with its painted ceilings, marble pillars and painted tile fountains was built to waft the movie-goer out of reality and into a Hollywood inspired dreamworld. Although built primarily for films, the California had a full sound stage, and many live acts were booked along with the films. As in all the theatres of this genre, the ubiquitous theatre organ concert preceded the show.

The California, rechristened the Fox after the war, remained the City's stellar movie house until 1950 and the opening of the Studio Theatre across the Street. The Studio's reign was shortlived, for by the mid-fifties television and the numerous drive-in theatres were drawing away the family-oriented generation of the post-war period. Unlike the Fox, the Studio has remained open as a Spanish language theatre.

*Crest Theatre 1959 (formerly the Victory).*
*Courtesy of Steve Levin.*

*Interior of the Theatre De Luxe. Photo taken from* Architect and Engineer, *1915. Courtesy of Jack Douglas.*

The so-called "adult" theatres made their appearance on First Street in the 70's. The Pussycat (now Camera I) was originally a shoe store which was remodeled as a theatre. Shortly after, the old Gay Theatre at the corner of First and San Salvador became an adult theatre and was renamed the Pussycat II.

Any recounting of downtown theatres would be incomplete without mention of the old Lyric Theatre which stood for almost 50 years across Second Street from the Jose. The neon sign from this long gone theatre resides in storage in the San Jose Historical Museum in Kelley Park. The Liberty Theatre, opened in 1914 and torn down in 1982, should also be remembered. It was the City's first Spanish language movie house. The salvaged remains of its ornate ceilings can be appreciated in the large new dining room at Teske's Germania on North First.

The list of lost theatres, the Victory, the Lyric, the Liberty and the Hippodrome form a ghostly pageant of pleasurable memories for a fading few who recall the Saturday matinees, bank nights, door prizes (wouldn't you like to have a complete set of the depression glass dinnerware now?), the chewy confections (Walnettoes, Black Crows, Jujubes, Holloway suckers), and the tears and the laughter of an innocent time and place.

# The Deluxe Theater:
# San Jose's First Movie Palace

SAN JOSE'S FIRST MOVIE PALACE, APPROPRIATELY called the Theatre De Luxe, was opened in August 1913. It was not the first theatre to show films. Moving pictures began to make their appearance in halls around the city in the late 1890's, at first sharing the bill with live vaudeville acts in such theaters as the Jose on South Second or the opera house called the Victory Theatre on North First. The Theatre De Luxe, however, was our first auditorium built specifically for film viewing.

Earlier movie houses, such as the legendary Sid Grauman's Unique Theater, were slapdash remodels of storefront properties. Built on one level with poor sightlines, these improvised theaters were cramped, stuffy and subject to fires. Had not Grauman's Unique on East Santa Clara Street been destroyed in the '06 earthquake, it might easily have joined the other victims of fires caused by overheated projection lamps or careless smokers. (Grauman must be credited, however, for being one of the first to ban smoking in his theater).

By 1913 it was becoming evident that the moving picture was here to stay. The flickering images, which were to remain silent until 1929, had revolutionized the entertainment business. Pioneer movie moguls such as Turner and Dahnken could see the potential of large profits in offering this seemingly endless variety of entertainment to the masses for as little as ten cents a ticket. This could only be done by building larger theaters and changing films as often as four times per week.

Turner and Dahnken, who controlled a chain of theaters in California, were determined to build one of the finest movie houses of its kind in San Jose. Designed by local architect William Binder, the Theatre De Luxe was also one of the largest structures of its kind. It was constructed on a rapidly expanding block of South First Street between San Antonio and San Carlos Streets. On the east side of the street, only the Central Market stood between the theater and the Twohy Building (now referred to as the Paseo Building — the Twohy and the Montgomery Hotel across the street are the only buildings left on the block from this era).

With its divided balcony and spacious orchestra, the theater could hold up to 1600 patrons. The high ceilings and the basement fans which could change the air every three minutes kept the auditorium from becoming stuffy in spite of the common practice of smoking stogies during the show. As one can see in the accompanying photo, the ample exterior fire escapes would probably have met even today's strict fire codes. Though they designed the theater for movie audiences, the developers did not wish to exclude the possibility of presenting live acts, so all of the usual backstage machinery, including fly lofts, lights and dressing rooms, were built in.

As the article in the *Mercury and Herald* edition of August 24, 1913 stated: *New Theatre De Luxe is splendid addition to architectural beauty of San Jose.* Designed in the style of the Italian Renaissance, it was indeed an impressive

*T&D Theatre De Luxe 1913.*

addition to the street. Not cluttered with all of the gaudy marquees, lights and signage of theaters of the late 20s and 30s, it had the classic appearance of an opera house or legitimate theater. Exterior lighting consisted of rows of lights which outlined the building and the oval windows. The lighted sunburst on the roof and the rectangular sign jutting out over the marquee, both of which can be seen in the photo, were later additions which heralded even more gross disfigurations to come.

Some of the first films shown at the T & D, as it was soon to be called, were: *Hearts Adrift* featuring "little Mary Pickford," *The Vicar of Wakefield* and *The Bride of Lammoor* (presumably based on the Walter Scott novel). In 1919 the T & D announced that it would present full one hour symphony concerts. In the first concert on February 9th, a thirty piece ensemble conducted by maestro Levi N. Harmon accompanied vocalists Ethelbert Nevin and Caroline Price in a selection of songs by Schubert, Sullivan and Puccini. The orchestra's big moment came with the closing William Tell overture. Along with this high class affair, and for only the price of a twenty cent ticket, one could also catch the film *The Romance of Tarzan*.

Competition from such mixed venue theaters as the Victory, Jose and the American Theatre just across the street, led the T & D to feature such live acts as the Fanchon and Marco dancing girls and the bands of Max Bradfield, Henry Santry and Ted Lewis. The T & D's giant organ, an essential element of the theater experience, was played by Charlie Hayward who would later become manager. After the theater was equipped for the talkies — the T & D was the first to show them — there were fewer live acts featured on the programs.

Changes of management and name are common in San Jose theater history, and the story of the Theatre De Luxe is no exception. In 1925 the T & D was taken over by Fox Theaters which changed the name to the California. In 1928 the Fox chain opened their new movie palace down in the next block and named it the California (now called the Fox), so they again renamed the old T & D the Fox Mission. With the newer Fox outlet down the street, the Mission got fewer of the first run features. One exception was the showing of *Gone With the Wind* which ran for a month — reputed to be the longest run for a film up to that time.

By the postwar period the fading Mission Theater was a second run house that occasionally ran revivals of old films. The first victim of the fickle audience that had turned to television, it closed its doors forever on July 4th, 1952. The final film was *The Little Big Horn*, the story of Custer's last stand, an irony not overlooked by Dick Barrett and the other news people who wrote about the theater's demise. It was demolished several years later and the First Western Bank and the House of Fabrics took its place.

It is hard to believe that the old De Luxe/Mission Theatre has been gone for almost as long as it stood on South First Street. It served the community well through two world wars and the Great Depression. Everyone who grew up in San Jose during that period must have known good times there. If it were standing today, it would be, like the Fox Theatre, a city landmark. It is, however, like most of the downtown of yesteryear, a fading memory.

Hester Theatre. Now the Towne.
Photo courtesy of Steve Levin.

# Our Neighborhood Theaters

WITH ALL THE INTEREST IN THE MOVIE PALACES OF the past, the California/Fox Theatre for example, it is easy to forget the humble neighborhood theatres. These little movie houses played an important role in introducing generations of young people to films.

Our first theaters were all located downtown. They were built for plays, vaudeville and other live acts, but by the 1920s moving pictures were becoming the major features. An attractive form of inexpensive entertainment, films could easily be shown in outlying districts, and as new neighborhoods developed, movie houses were some of the first community structures.

San Jose's first neighborhood theater, the Hester, was built about 1928. Located at 1433 The Alameda at the corner of Hester Avenue, it would serve the developing Hanchett Park and Rosegarden neighborhoods. It was designed by the local firm of architects, Binder and Curtis, and was constructed on the site of the Victor Benson garage.

Almost immediately, the Hester had to cope with talking pictures. It was refitted for sound with the latest RCA photophone projectors, and ten thousand square feet of balsam wood soundproofing material was applied to the walls. The grand reopening took place on May 1, 1930. The *Mercury Herald* ad announced in bold letters: *Hester Theatre opens with Talking Pictures, talking as you've never heard them talk before! Hail to the first one: Joan Crawford in Untamed with big surrounding program!... Adults 30 cents, children 10 cents.*

The Hester competed successfully with the downtown movie houses, generally appealing to mature audiences in their choice of films. In 1949 it was renamed the Towne. A major change occurred in 1955 when Mason Shaw, owner of the Saratoga, Burbank and Gay theaters, took it over and turned it into a specialty house featuring foreign and art films. For many years the Towne was the only place to see British comedies starring Alec Guinness and Peter Sellers. The French film, *A Man and a Woman,* turned out to be what was probably the longest running film in San Jose's history.

Mason Shaw introduced the sexually explicit Danish film *I Am Curious Yellow* in 1969 and was promptly closed down. The landmark court decision which allowed such films to be shown started the wave of "adult movies" which soon engulfed even the sedate Towne. It remained an "adults only" theater until it closed several years ago.

The Camera Cinemas, under the leadership of James Zuur, have refurbished the old theater. It has recently reopened again as an outlet for first run foreign films, U.S. made independent films and kids' matinees.

Our second neighborhood theater was called the Willow Glen. Opened in 1933 at 1350 Lincoln Avenue (on the east side of the street near Minnesota), it was built by the same group that owned the Hester. Also designed by Binder and Curtis in Spanish style, it was only half the size of the Hester — about 400

*Mexico Theatre. Photo courtesy of Dennis Skaggs.*

seats. In 1949 the management changed the name to the Vogue and began specializing in opera and dance films. It closed forever in 1950.

James B. Lima, local movie mogul who owned the Jose, Liberty, Gay and Crest, felt that there was a need for another theater on Lincoln Avenue. The result was the Garden which opened on June 22, 1949 with the Humphrey Bogart classic *Knock on Any Door*. Designed by O.A. Deichman of San Francisco, this 1,000 seat epitome of large postwar cinemas featured rocking chair loge seating, the latest in air conditioning and indirect lighting. Lavishly appointed, the auditorium was decorated with massive murals depicting the industrial and agricultural growth of our valley. Murals on either side of the proscenium incorporated bas-relief figures set on a brilliantly colored floral background.

As a large single screen theater the Garden has, from the beginning, had an uphill battle to remain economically viable. After running for some years as a Spanish language film house, it closed, and has been converted into office and commercial space. The classic sign and marquee remain.

While the Garden was being planned, a less ambitious neighborhood theater was being built on East Santa Clara Street at 25th. Dubbed the Mayfair for the district in which it was located, the 800 seat theater opened May 20, 1949, with the premiere of Howard Hawk's classic *Red River* starring John Wayne and Montgomery Clift. The *Mercury* ads on opening week boasted several theater firsts: *a cry room for the convenience of mothers with restless children ... a processed weather plant ... air purification germ killer so there is no need to worry about catching someone else's cold ... cycloramic screen, 20% more light ... first theatre fountain.*

The Mayfair, owned and operated by Arthur Yaramie, was, for many years, a successful second run film house which catered to eastsiders and San Jose State students. The Yaramies sold out to Affiliated Theaters Inc. in 1962 and the name was changed to the Esquire. When Jose Borges, owner of the Mexico Theatre on Market Street (formerly the Liberty) was forced to make way for downtown redevelopment, he acquired the Esquire and renamed it the Mexico, and it now shows exclusively Spanish language films.

Not to be outdone by Willow Glen, the unincorporated district of Burbank opened its opulent new theater at 550 San Jose-Los Gatos Road (now Bascom) on September 5, 1951 with the film *On Moonlight Bay* starring Doris Day and Gordon McRae. The timing could not have been worse, as television and drive-in theaters were drawing attendance away from the big theaters. The Burbank has had a history of closings, reopenings and changes of format, and it may now have the dubious distinction of being Santa Clara County's last "adult film" house.

Our neighborhood theaters met a particular need as San Jose was growing. Several generations enjoyed their intimacy and convenience. Film goers of today are faced with the prospect of attending the multi-screen complex with the giant snackbar lobby or the sterile shoebox in the shopping mall. Restorations such as the Hester/Towne will allow us to again experience the quality and atmosphere of an earlier day.

*Towne Theatre. Photo courtesy of Michael Selic.*

# Our Binder and Curtis Buildings

*Postcard of Antler Grill Elk's Building San Jose, California*

WE HAVE WITNESSED THE DEVELOPMENT OF A whole new cityscape in downtown San Jose — new hotels, theaters, banks and office towers. Most of the plans for these buildings came from architects who practice beyond the boundaries of Santa Clara County. This building boom is not the first in this century; it merely replaces the results of an earlier downtown renaissance which occurred between 1900 and the Great Depression of 1929.

The prime mover in the earlier development of downtown was the local real estate tycoon T.S. Montgomery (1855-1944). He needed a talented architect to fulfill his vision and he found one in William Binder.

William Binder (pronounced Bender), a native of San Francisco, began his career as an apprentice draftsman in 1890. He polished his skills working for the prominent local architect G.W. Page until setting out on his own in 1897. For the next 57 years his name would appear on the blueprints of many of our City's landmark buildings. In 1918 he made his talented young assistant Ernest N. Curtis a partner in the firm which would thenceforth be known as Binder and Curtis.

*First Street postcard from the collection of Jack Douglas.*

*Commercial Building, San Jose, California*

Only a fraction of the Binder and Curtis structures have survived the ravages of time and urban renewal, but those which are left are significant City landmarks which have been or are soon to be restored. To give the reader a feeling for the types of structures that Binder and Curtis designed and to jog the memories of old timers who may have forgotten our pre-war City, here is a chronological account of some of the buildings.

One of Binder's first projects was the renovation of the old St. James Hotel which stood until the 1930s when it was razed to make way for the Post Office. In 1903 he won the bid to design the Carnegie library building on Washington Square, and a year later he did the plans for the Jose Theater. This distinctive vaudeville-turned-movie house is our oldest theater.

A bigger project was the old Hall of Justice at Market and St. James. This sandstone structure was hardly finished when the '06 quake knocked off many of its more decorative elements. Perhaps the most significant Binder building was the 1907 Garden City Bank Building at South First and San Fernando. It was our first steel-framed skyscraper (7 stories), and it would become the headquarters for T.S. Montgomery enterprises. Before its destruction in the early 1970s, it

housed the Wells Fargo offices. However, it was historically significant for another event: the establishment, by Dr. Charles Herrold in 1909, of the world's first regularly transmitting radio station.

The Art Nouveau style Douglas apartment building was built at South First and San Carlos in 1908. Considered too far from the center of town at the time, it signalled the beginning of the City's march southward. The Mission style firehouse at 61 North Third also came from Binder's drawing board that year. To further solidify his holdings on South First, Montgomery had Binder design the hotel (1911) on the corner of San Antonio which still bears the developer's name.

1913 was a big year for Binder's firm. Projects included the Elks Building, the YMCA, the DeLuxe Theater and the Burrell Building. The Elks Building at North First and St. John was a center for many of the town's social activities for four decades. The old YMCA Building at Third and Santa Clara stood empty for over 30 years until it was recently renovated for banking and offices. The DeLuxe Theater, known as the Mission Theater when it was razed in the 1950s, was our first theater designed for motion pictures. This movie house and the adjoining Burrell Building helped fill in the 200 block of South First.

Garden City Bank Building,
San Jose, California.

In 1917 Binder and Curtis provided plans for a second skyscraper, the Twohy Building, across from the Montgomery Hotel. This five-story office tower was once the location of many of the town's doctors and dentists. Also appearing that year was the Sunsweet office building at San Antonio and Market.

1919 saw the addition of their American Theater at 261 South First. This theater underwent two name changes, the State and the U.A., before it was razed in the late 70s. The ten-story Commercial Building on North First was the big project for 1926. The top two stories of this still impressive building housed the facilities of the Commercial Club, an important meeting place for the Valley's businessmen until 1934. The entire building was taken over as the headquarters for the Seventh Army during World War II. In 1926 Binder and Curtis also designed the addition to the San Jose Hospital. Projects completed before the downturn of the Depression were the Mausoleum at Oak Hill Cemetery, the Hester/Towne Theater and the Willow Glen Theater.

T.S. Montgomery contracted with out-of-town architects for all of his buildings south of San Carlos, which included the California/Fox Theater, the Sainte Claire Hotel and the Sainte Claire Building, but he returned to Binder and Curtis for the Civic Auditorium in 1934. This was Montgomery's most important contribution to the city and the capstone for the architectural firm.

Few would claim that any of our early architects, Binder and Curtis included, were highly original or trend setting, but they worked with great skill in producing a multitude of pleasing designs in a variety of styles that put a stamp of distinction on our City. San Jose is finally mature enough to realize that it must integrate the best of the past in order to create a unique and appealing environment. William Binder and Ernest Curtis should be remembered for their considerable contribution.

## Christian Assembly/Petit Trianon

Anyone who wants to see a good example of one of William Binder's buildings needs to go no further than the old Christian Assembly Church on North Fifth Street.

The Christian Assembly practiced a form of healing somewhat akin to Christian Science. Not long after the church was built, Binder, who suffered from chronic headaches, subjected himself to their treatments and was cured. The church gave up its location in 1982 in order to consolidate with their Willow Glen parish.

This gem of a building has been recently refurbished by Keith Watt who purchased it to be the headquarters of Mother Olson's Inns. Renamed The Petit Trianon, it still looks exactly as it did in 1923 when Binder designed it. The reception hall is a warm balconied room with a large fireplace and graceful stairways. The main sanctuary/auditorium is nicely appointed and makes an excellent hall for concerts, films and other events.

*Photo by Jack Douglas.*

# Aestheticism Comes to San Jose

IT IS AMAZING HOW QUICKLY TRENDS IN STYLE AND fashion sweep the country and the world, and then are quickly passed over when the next wave hits the shore. Even without the help of radio and television, the citizens of the pioneer city of San Jose were influenced by the ideas of a small group of artists and intellectuals halfway around the world in England. I am speaking in particular about the changes in style of our local "Victorian" houses. During the reign of Victoria, (1837-1901) a series of architectural styles evolved in England, and were shortly copied or modified for use in America. All were unquestionably accepted by builders and home-owners in frontier San Jose.

The earliest was the Gothic style (1840-1860), later came the Italian Renaissance style (1860-1880), then an even more ornate hybrid variation referred to as the Stick or Eastlake style (1870-1900), the Queen Anne (1880-1910), and lastly, the Craftsman style (1890-1914).

The changes in taste and style (fads and fash-ions?) were the direct result of a wave of artistic and aesthetic theories, a reaction to the crasser effects of the industrialization, that swept England during the reign of Victoria. The popular writer and critic John Ruskin, along with the Pre-Raphaelite Brotherhood (artists and poets which included the Rossetti's, William Morris and others) started the movement off by extolling the many moral and artistic virtues of the Middle Ages.

By the 1870s, the Italian Renaissance became the high ideal as defined by the art critic Walter Pater and the members of the Aesthetic Movement who believed in "art for its own sake," a radical idea in the era of pragmatism. The excesses of Oscar Wilde who, to some, personified the aesthetic movement, were paro-died by Gilbert and Sullivan in their popular operetta, "Patience, or Bunthorne's Bride." In the play, Bunthorne, the Wildeian aesthetic poet, admits he's a sham, and recites a list of aesthetic ideals of the move-ment to which he no longer subscribes:

*Let me confess!*
*A languid love of lillies does not blight me!*
*Lank limbs and haggard cheeks do not delight me!*
*I do not care for dirty greens*
*By any means*
*I do not long for all one sees*
*that's Japanese*
*I am not fond of uttering platitudes*
*In stained glass attitudes*
*In short, my medievalism's affectation*
*Born of a morbid love of admiration*

and later in the patter song that follows, Bunthorne states:

*...you will rank as an apostle in the high aesthetic band, if you walk down Piccadilly with a poppy or a Lilly in your Medieval hand.*

A British humorist described an aesthetic interior: "in which the young intellectual woman could safely relax and lend a properly attentive ear to the patter of Pater and whispers of Wilde, as one decorated with pendant Japanese fans. The cast iron mantelpiece, tastefully incised with sunflowers by Mr. Walter Crane, supported two Chinese ginger jars and a vase of Satsuma ware in which a solitary lily bore witness to the high regard in which the Oriental ideals of flower arrangement were now held."

Wilde toured the U.S. in 1882, sponsored by the American producers of "Patience." On April 3rd of that year, Oscar lectured to San Joseans on the importance of home decoration. The talk, given at the California Theatre on South Second Street, was only moderately well attended. Journalists were naturally more comfortable writing about Oscar's appearance than in dealing with the subject matter of his talk. Wilde encouraged this by offering up rather dull fare in a not particularly interesting presentation. The writer for the *Mercury* describes him thus:

*For before the audience stood a most grotesque boyish-looking young man, whose dress may have been modeled after that of dead and gone aesthetes of some forgotten age, but which was, nevertheless, the most atrociously ugly suit of wearing apparel that could well be devised by man. A suit of dark velvet, with sombre suggestiveness of having been buried for a century or more...the coat was rounded and short, the vest exposed a liberal area of shirtfront and knee breeches met a pair of thin black stockings, through which showed another pair of white ones.* (This writer was obviously in the front row!)

The *Mercury* reporter clearly had his own standards for what constituted an aesthetic individual, and Oscar didn't fit the bill:

*When we come to his face we see a heavy set countenance, devoid of all the mobile shades of expression which one would naturally associate with aesthetic aspirations and a poetic soul. A countenance that gives little or no evidence of the strong intellect and clear understanding of the man. A rather low but intellectual brow, a straight long nose, and large mouth, set with large disagreeable teeth, form a not very pleasant whole. There is something in his dark eyes however, which redeems this lack of beauty.*

Oscar, who engendered hoots and catcalls in the mining camps (where he gained the miners' respect by drinking them all under the table), and in less civilized cities such as Stockton and San Francisco, found the staid citizens of San Jose proper and attentive, or as the *Mercury* reported the next day: *The audience throughout the evening expressed neither pleasure or displeasure, but listened in respectful and decorous silence to what the lecturer had to say.* After such a sobering experience, Wilde probably went out afterward for a tall glass of General Henry M. Naglee's famous local brandy.

One wonders if anyone in the crowd, who mainly gathered to see the controversial Wilde in his green velvet pantaloons, ever associated Wilde's ideals and the ornate Gothic, Italianate and Queen Anne homes they lived in. Wilde must have been impressed to see so many lavish Victorian-style homes in what he expected to be a rustic frontier. Could the dreamy poets of the Pre-Raphaelite movement ever have imagined, in their most extravagant flights of fancy, that the ideals of aestheticism would ever find the way to San Jose?

*Oscar Wilde. A New York trade card of the time, showing Wilde in one of his lecturing costumes. From* Oscar Wilde: Irish Poets and Poetry of the Nineteenth Century *by Robert D. Pepper.*

# Our Craftsman Heritage

A LATER STYLE OF ARCHITECTURE, THE CRAFTSMAN bungalow, came to America as a result of the Arts and Crafts Movement in England. A predominant style in San Jose between 1890 and the Great War (1914), many well preserved examples can be found all over town, particularly in Naglee Park, Hanchett Park and the Rosegarden areas.

The craftsman ideal can be traced back to the well-known artist and writer William Morris (1834-1896), who moved beyond the elitist medieval manifestations of the Pre-Raphaelites into an idealized form of socialism which attempted to revive the simple values of a preindustrial society. This new society would give up their machine-made goods for homespun cloth, homebaked bread and handcrafted household articles. The cottage industry of a Silas Marner was to be preferred over the future of Jules Verne.

The architectural outgrowth of this revolutionary idea was the ideal peasant cottage or bungalow which would be constructed of native materials. The key to the new style was economy and craftsmanship. Cobblestones were laid up in the foundations, fireplaces, chimneys and porches. Walls, whether stucco, frame or shingle, were stained or painted in earthen shades. The roofs, with their wide overhangs, displaying exposed rafters and knee braces, were generally of wood shingle. Ideally, the craftsman home would be simple enough to be built by its owner. Sears and Roebuck capitalized on this concept in the U.S. by marketing craftsman homes in kit form.

Unlike the earlier Victorian architectural tastemakers, Morris believed that the new generation had to go beyond the exterior decoration of the Gothic Italianate or Queen Anne homes in order to make the home a vital part of the life of the owner. As a result of this philosophy, Morris used his artistic skill to design appropriate interiors for the new (old) style. Since the homes were small, many features such as built-in cupboards, window seats, shelves and closets eliminated the necessity of clumsy chairs, chests of drawers, bookcases and wardrobes. The center attraction of the craftsman home was its cobblestone or clinker brick fireplace. Inglenooks, the built-in fireside seating, symbolized the family relationship with "hearth and home." It is this homey feel, whether real or idealized, that makes the craftsman home a joy to live in. Craftsmanship is reflected on the inside by the natural wood paneling or wainscoting in the halls and dining rooms, the beamed ceilings, the use of stained and leaded glass, and the many metal crafted light fixtures and other hardware. The use of tile in the bathroom and kitchen gives each home an individual flavor.

Morris went into the home furnishings business, creating many unique items such as the Morris chair, Morris wallpapers (now being recreated for Victorian buffs by a firm in Benicia) and other items which used natural materials, fibers, stained glass, etc.

In America, the movement was taken up by Gustav Stickley whose *Craftsman Magazine* (1901-1916), albeit more philosophical, was the equivalent of our own *Sunset or Better Homes and Gardens*. Stickley spearheaded a building boom which was an early manifestation of the concept of the "American Dream" of an aesthetically attractive, small home for every man and his family. He stressed the democratic values of home ownership, pride in workmanship and the family. As the movement progressed, Stickley began to assimilate some of the elements of the California mission style into his drawings.

Stickley characterized his craftsman mission furniture as "straight lined, hand-finished, well-made furniture, constructed on primitive lines and planned for comfort, durability and beauty and expressing the true spirit of democracy." These heavy pieces, which were, in my childhood, relegated to back porches, summer cottages and attics, have recently become sought-after items on the antique market. There were many imitations massed-produced by other manufacturers, but the authentic pieces have the distinct woodworker's compass logo and motto "Als ik kan" (as I can) stamped on the underside.

Architects in San Francisco such as Bernard Maybeck, Julia Morgan, Ernest Coxhead, and Willis Polk used many of the ideas of the arts and crafts movement to create a hybrid style known in the architectural history books as the San Francisco Bay Tradition. A group of artists, writers and Berkeley professors under the influence of Maybeck created an arts and crafts colony north of the UC campus known as the Hilltop Club. Here they espoused a simple life that included an appreciation of art in a natural setting. And what could be a more appropriate place than in the Berkeley Hills where one could watch the sun go down over the Golden Gate? Their clubhouse and most of their homes were products of Maybeck's

genius. Unfortunately the Berkeley fire of 1923 swept up the hills and destroyed their dream. Many homes were rebuilt, and along with the examples in San Francisco and the Peninsula, represent the West's first original architectural style.

San Francisco artists Arthur and Lucia Mathews followed the lead of Morris and Stickley by setting up a shop which produced craftsman style furnishings of redwood with designs which depict many of the natural wonders of this region.

New families who are moving back into our historic neighborhoods are rediscovering the charm of these homey dwellings. Thanks to our mild climate and the care of the previous generation, the craftsman bungalows in San Jose are some of the finest examples in the nation (the illustration of the Martin Avenue bungalows shown on the previous page is from the book: *What Style Is It?* which was published in Washington, D.C. by the Preservation Press). We can take pride in the fact that the spirit of the arts and crafts movement is alive and well in San Jose.

# University of Pacific Legacy

KOSTKA HALL AT BELLARMINE PREPARATORY School was torn down on April 9, 1987. The handsome Mission style dormitory, built in 1909, was originally named Helen Guth Hall. Its primary significance was that it was one of the remaining structures left from the days when the campus of the University of the Pacific occupied the site.

The University of the Pacific campus was an important educational and cultural institution in our area from 1850 until 1925 when it was moved to Stockton. Perhaps a bit of UOP history is in order here to put this in perspective.

Before 1850, the closest thing San Jose had to an institution of higher learning was Reverend Edward Bannister's English and Classical School, later known as the San Jose Academy. Its first classes were given in a building at the southeast corner of Second and San Fernando Streets. Reverend Bannister was given a charge by the Methodist Church to form the first college in California. This college, originally chartered as the California

Central Dining Hall, c. 1886. San Jose Historical Museum Collections.

Wesleyan College on July 10, 1851, and later renamed the University of the Pacific, can lay claim to be California's first official school of higher education. Later that same year, the Mission School in Santa Clara, and the College of Notre Dame (then located in San Jose) were chartered, making the Santa Clara Valley the center of higher education in the West.

The first University of the Pacific buildings were built in Santa Clara on Main Street across from City Park. There were only two: the Female Collegiate Institute and the Men's Collegiate Institute, thus forming the first semi-coeducational school in the state. The students lived and studied in their respective buildings so that Victorian decorum could be maintained. The Archanian (men's) and Emendiah (women's) Literary Societies were formed in 1854 and 1858 respectively, making them the first such groups in the West. The UOP medical school was formed in San Francisco in 1859 and still operates today as a dental school.

In the early years, when California was cut off from the eastern United States, the prospective students in the West had no choice but to attend the colleges in our valley. With the opening of the transcontinental railroad, however, students from well-to-do families could go east to more prestigious and better endowed colleges and universities. As a consequence, the universities and colleges here set about expanding and modernizing their campuses. In 1866, UOP purchased 435 acres of land on two tracts between San Jose and Santa Clara for $72,000. The land, formerly part of the El Potrero de Santa Clara Rancho and the old Stockton Ranch, was divided into two sections, one for the university and the other into residential lots which were sold to support the university.

Located in an unincorporated area, the new campus required a postal address. University officials hoped to use the name University Park, but discovered that this title was already registered to the University of Southern California, so they had to settle for the name College Park. A short time later the Southern Pacific established their College Park Station adjacent to the campus. The name was prophetic, for in the early part of this century, then president William Guth convinced the trustees that it was presumptuous to call their institution a university, so the name was changed to College of the Pacific.

It was not until 1961, when the Stockton campus had expanded greatly, that the name reverted.

The opening of the railroad and the ability of students to go east was only the beginning of UOP's problems in maintaining enrollments, for other colleges and universities were also springing up in the vicinity. In 1870, the first State Normal School was built on Washington Square in San Jose, and in 1891 the first classes at Leland Stanford University had commenced. The beautiful new Stanford campus was even then almost a "world class" institution and a magnet for the best and brightest of the state's youth. UOP struggled with its financing as the economic ups and downs of the late 19th century took a toll.

The enrollment picture improved somewhat when, in 1895, it was agreed to incorporate another Methodist affiliated school, Napa College, into UOP. The residents of Napa were not happy about losing their college but the weight of economics prevailed.

Another significant event took place with the opening of the commodious Music Conservatory Building on the College Park Campus in 1890. The music department had been organized in 1878 under the guidance of Professor F. Loui King, who, in the past decade had developed it into a full-fledged school known as the Pacific Conservatory of Music.

King left UOP in 1893 to form the King

*East Hall building at the College of the Pacific. San Jose Historical Museum Collections.*

*Helen Guth Hall, c. 1915. Photo courtesy of Holt-Atherton Center for Western Studies, University of the Pacific.*

Conservatory in San Jose, however the Conservatory continued to flourish under other directors, including, in 1919, the noted American composer Howard Hanson.

At the turn of the century, the College Park campus consisted of five buildings. West Hall, built in 1871, was the ladies dormitory, and the Levi-Goodrich designed East Hall was the men's dormitory. Central Hall held the classrooms, library and dining room. There were also the Jackson-Goodstall Astronomical Observatory and the new Romanesque Music Conservatory building.

The destruction caused by the 1906 earthquake dealt the struggling institution its most severe blow. Damage was so extensive to East Hall that the fourth floor had to be removed in the renovation. Other buildings were significantly damaged as well. A miracle worker was needed if the school was to be rebuilt and its shaky financial situation improved. Such a one was found in the person of William Wesley Guth who was installed as president in 1908. Dr. Guth, a native of San Francisco who dropped his ministerial duties in Cambridge Massachusetts to come west,

wasted no time in patching up the old and planning for the new on the UOP campus.

High on his list of building priorities were a new ladies dormitory, a gymnasium, a science hall, a library and a president's home. When Dr. Guth left in 1913 to become president of Goucher College in Maryland, most of these goals had been accomplished. The most impressive new structure, the ladies dormitory, was named for his wife Helen Guth.

More important perhaps, was the impact Dr. Guth had on the quality of education at the college. Enrollments doubled during his regime, and a firm fiscal foundation was established.

During this period, serious thought was being given to finding a better location for the college. The growth of San Jose had pressed in around College Park and the proximity to the noisy railroad was leading some trustees to believe that it was time to move. Obviously, President Guth was committed to improving the College Park campus, and his relatively short tenure may have been due to disagreements with the trustees over this issue.

Several other catastrophes occurred which

turned the tide for the move. Central Hall, the primary classroom building (which also held the kitchen and dining room) burned to the ground in 1914. Not long after, West Hall burned, destroying the library and requiring the science department and other classrooms to be moved to East Hall.

After World War I, attempts at relocation were resumed and a suitable location was found on the outskirts of Stockton. By 1925, construction of the new campus was complete and classes began.

It is important to remember that California's first established institution of higher learning was once located in this valley. During its seventy years here, many of UOP's graduates went on to become leaders in our community and the west. Through its programs, particularly the Pacific Conservatory of Music, it provided a cultural stimulus which was much needed in our frontier society.

The demolition of Kostka/Guth Hall removes one more link with this illustrious chapter in our past. Soon only place names such as University Avenue and College Park will remain to remind us of this unique part of our history.

# The King Conservatory of Music/ Germania Hall

FOR OVER SIXTY YEARS, GERMANIA HALL HAS served as the social and cultural club of San Jose's German population. Among the earliest European settlers in the Pueblo of San Jose, they formed the Germania Verein (society) here in 1856. For many years, the Hall was for the exclusive use of the members and their guests, and many native San Joseans probably had their first authentic German food in the Hall's dining room. More recently, Germania Hall has opened its doors to the public, and offers a wide variety of German cuisine for lunches and dinners.

The spacious hall, with its second floor gallery, was originally built to house the King Conservatory of Music. Named after its founder, F. Loui King, the Conservatory was one of the leading cultural and educational institutions in San Jose between 1895 and 1920. F. Loui King (the "F" stood for Frank) came from Oregon to San Jose in the early nineties to take charge of the music department of the University of the Pacific, then in College Park off the Alameda.

Soon the Maestro had the support of many of the county's leading citizens in establishing the King Conservatory of Music. Such men as: Stanford President David Starr Jordan, President Morris E. Dailey of the Normal School, S.B. Hunkins of the Garden City Bank, real estate developer T.S. Montgomery and others were prominent members of the Conservatory's boards. Professor King cer-

*The King Conservatory of Music. Photo from* Sunshine, Fruit and Flowers.

tainly didn't lack vision when he stated: *I am convinced that at San Jose or at Stanford University (King obviously wanted to keep his options open) there is a possibility of building up the greatest musical center in America, if not the world; a center that in a few years can be made not less illustrious than Bayreuth, and that will attract to this valley the best artists and the most ardent students of music of all nations. To effect this, we have the climate, the location, the cultured community, the native talent and all the elements out of which a musical center must be made. There needs nothing to realize the result but the money and the men.*

The Conservatory occupied a matching pair of two-story Victorians (only one still remains) and the custom built Hall which was designed by local Architect F.D. Wolfe. This auditorium which had a seating capacity of 500, also included nine small studios and two larger choral rooms. The two houses provided further music rooms, a well-stocked library and living quarters for King, his wife and their three children.

Students came from several western states to attend the Conservatory and at least one, the daughter of Garden City Bank President Hunkins, went on to study in Europe with the great Polish/German pianist Moritz Moszkowski. The Conservatory catalogues never failed to reproduce a letter of endorsement from Moszkowski, thanking King for preparing Miss Hunkins so well.

*Germania Hall today. Photo courtesy of Jack Douglas.*

The King Conservatory certainly served as a focus for the small San Jose community's cultural life. The San Jose Symphony, reputed to be the oldest in the state, used the facilities for rehearsals and concerts, and the Conservatory orchestra, with Maestro King at the piano, gave frequent concerts for the locals. As Eugene Sawyer states in his *History of Santa Clara County: the air was charged with music with (J.H.) Ellwood and King in town ... their orchestra furnished San Jose some of the best music it had ever listened to.*

King, who was touted as a composer, musician and teacher, was dean of a faculty with impressive credentials. Many of them had studied in Europe. Mrs. King was an assistant teacher of instrumental music, and all three children were pupils at the Conservatory. Their daughter Luena won laurels as a performer and composer, and their son Frank G. King rose to become the managing director of the school during its final years. The third child, Loui F. King, became a local attorney.

The Conservatory could not continue however, without the inspiration of the Maestro, and faded away shortly after his death in 1914. King Conservatory — Germania Hall is an institution with deep roots in the cultural history of this community. How wonderful it must have been for the early citizens of San Jose to have had this resource, and how marvelous it is that we can still enjoy its benefits and its heritage.

# San Jose's Forgotten Private Parks

A HOLE IN THE GROUND ON KEYES STREET is all that remains of the old Cedar Brook Park. This longtime San Jose recreation area, which was located across the street north of Happy Hollow, is a reminder of the many other early parks which are now only part of our history.

Cedar Brook, on the shady banks of Coyote Creek, was, at the turn of the century, just far enough out on the edge of town to qualify as wilderness. When the electric trolley made its terminus there in 1907, it became a popular place for picnics, birthday parties and other social events.

Like many of our early parks, Cedar Brook was owned and operated by private enterprise. Although the early city fathers had set aside park land for Washington and St. James Squares, funds were not immediately found to landscape them properly. Perhaps the development of the popular privately owned parks contributed to this inaction.

The earliest local privately owned botanical gardens were on the estates of General Naglee and Louis Prevost. Naglee's was occasionally open to view, but Prevost, a French nurseryman, opened his gardens on the Guadalupe River south of San Carlos Street to the public in the 1850s. Prevost's failed attempts to introduce the silkworm into this country caused him to lose his property in 1860.

Prevost's northern neighbor, Antonio Sunol, turned his riverside property located between San

Carlos and Santa Clara Streets into a recreation area known as Live Oak Park (the site of the recently proposed Guadalupe River Park). The river at Live Oak Park became San Jose's official swimming hole when Mayor Thomas Monahan placed a dam at the juncture of the Guadalupe and Los Gatos Creek, thereby creating Lake Monahan. Live Oak Park fell before the developers in 1919.

Two other popular parks made accessible by the trolley line were Schuetzen Park and Driving Park. Schuetzen was on the west side of Monterey Road just beyond Oak Hill Cemetery. Its primary attraction was its German beer garden and shooting range. Driving Park was just across the road in the area that later became the county fairgrounds. It was so-called because of the automobile and horse races held there. Both of these parks were abandoned by 1913, and the loss of fares due to their closure resulted in the discontinuance of the trolley on Monterey Road.

The most elaborate private parks to be developed in San Jose were O'Donnell's Gardens and the Hanchett Santa Clara Railroad Company's amusement center known as Luna Park.

William O'Donnell, who emigrated from Ireland in 1852, was a nurseryman by profession and a member of the city council in the early 1860s. He turned his nursery and orchard (located between Ninth, Tenth, Reed and William Streets) into a private park known as O'Donnell's Gardens. It became one of the most popular recreational places in pioneer San Jose. It was, at first, primarily a botanical showplace, but O'Donnell continually added new attractions such as a zoo, a dancing pavilion, a skating rink and an observatory. The grounds included lakes and ponds filled with fish, grottoes and shady nooks for lovers. So popular was this spot that a horsecar line was extended down Ninth Street from Santa Clara Street to transport the throngs of visitors. The local paper relates a giant festival held there to celebrate the nation's centennial on July 4, 1876. We have yet to uncover a list of the variety of zoological specimens housed in the park, but we do know there were sea lions. O'Donnell's Gardens faded into history after the death of the founder in 1883.

*Circa 1910, Port San Say on the Guadalupe River.*
*San Jose Historical Museum Collections.*

---

*Luna Park Grandstand. Courtesy of Jack Douglas.*

Lewis E. Hanchett had no romantic notions of the importance of nature. His Luna Park, located at North 18th Street (then 14th Street) and Berryessa offered thrills and amusement to the people of San Jose and lots of riders for his network of streetcars.

At the start of the project in 1907, the *Mercury's* headlines shouted: *Nothing spared in perfecting Luna Park ... new pleasure grounds to be among finest in state — theater, plunge, rink, zoo and midway included in calculations of constructors — management.* The article included sketches of the proposed theater with 4,000 seats to be designed by the local firm of Wolfe and McKenzie. Some projects were slow to materialize (the theater never did) but the grandstand provided cover for the many spectators who came for baseball games, balloon ascensions and early air shows. The park opened officially in 1910 under the supervision of Audley Ingersoll Amusement Company. The amusements featured the Scenic Railway (an early roller coaster), the Water Mill (a boat water slide) and the most popular, a five-story tower with a polished wooden spiral chute called the Devil's Slide.

For the sedate there was the dance pavilion which the management assured: *will be conducted in a most orderly manner. The regulations will be as strict as any enforced at first class dances.* A large cafe building was equipped to serve meals at all hours. Hanchett bought extra trolleys from Sacramento in order to carry in the customers during peak periods at a rate of one car every four minutes.

After its initial success, Luna Park began to decline. This loss of momentum probably brought about Hanchett's sale of his Santa Clara Railroad to Southern Pacific in 1911.

Luna Park had a brief new lease on life with the organization of the San Jose Roundup in 1915. The Roundups were four day rodeos which took place on and around the 4th of July. (See the chapter on The Roundup for a full account.) The whole town, and many people from all over the state turned out for these extravaganzas. The last Roundup in 1918 sig-

naled the end of the trail for Luna Park. A headline in the *Mercury* for July 20, 1920 said it all: *Famous ball park now factory site. Name "Luna Park" changed to "Industrial City" by Axle Corporation. After 12 years as sporting and pleasure resort, park re-dedicated to industry.*

Free enterprise brought the citizens of San Jose the first parks for recreation and amusement, but when the value of the land increased, the parks all fell to developers. (Frontier Village and Marine World are two recent examples.) It was only when local government got serious about not only setting aside park land but developing and maintaining it that the public could be assured of pleasant places to relax and recreate. San Jose's parks, private and public, have been a source of pride to its citizenry and have added to our image as the "Garden City."

## A SEA LION ON HIS TRAVELS

Last Saturday night or early on Sunday morning, the largest of the sea lions escaped from the inclosure at O'Donnell's Garden by climbing over the picket fence which is five feet high, and after hobbling through the grounds, climbed over the fence into William Street, and meandered down to the corner of Ninth Street, turned northward on the road to salt water. About 5 o'clock in the morning, a gentleman coming into the city saw him floundering along the road near Ninth and Empire, almost a mile from home. The gentleman notified Mr. O'Donnell of the fact, and the latter immediately started after the sea lion. The trail was visible nearly all the way to where he had been last seen, but upon arrival at that point he could not be found. Here was a dilemma; six hundred dollars worth of an amphibious monster gone, and all traces lost. While O'Donnell and his assistants were cogitating on their next move, a gentleman came up and informed them that he had the sea lion in his yard. The animal had gone out Empire Street until he came to a ditch which he entered, and was proceeding on his course to the bay, when discovered and driven into the yard. From there the owner had him driven into the road, and he was made to retrace his steps to his old abode in the garden. He reached home about 10 o'clock having traveled about three miles, considerably fatigued by the trip. Steps have been taken to prevent future escape.

*San Jose Mercury*

# The Alum Rock Park Log Cabin

THE LITTLE LOG CABIN AT ALUM ROCK PARK SITS alone and forgotten in its wooded setting. Gone are the natatorium, merry-go-round, dance pavilion, zoo and the endless picnic tables that accommodated thousands in the years gone by.

Unused and in a state of disrepair, the cabin was considered surplus by the Parks administration, and in 1974 it was written off by the Landmarks Commission as of no historical value.

However, it was not until 1982 that the Parks people became serious about actually tearing it down.

The proposal was routinely brought before the Landmarks Commission again for confirmation. This time the Commission decided that the cabin should be saved and made an official city landmark.

One could easily say that this about-face was typical of the vagaries of our volunteer boards and commissions, but it was instead a reflection of a major change in attitude about what is important about our past. Not long ago those who made decisions about our history were content to preserve only the memory of our past. When economics seemed to

*Log Cabin in Alum Rock Park. Photo courtesy of Jack Douglas.*

dictate that a structure was out of date or too expensive to restore, it was acceptable to remove it. If it had really been significant, a historic sign was placed on the empty site.

Fortunately the Alum Rock Log Cabin was not standing in the immediate way of progress. (The Murphy Building, the old city hall and a number of other important downtown historic structures were not so fortunate.) Not all of the Landmarks commissioners were convinced at first that the cabin would meet the city's criteria, based on the National Register of Historic Places guidelines, to be considered significant. Research into the humble building's history turned up a wealth of interesting details however.

Not an actual pioneer structure, the cabin was built through the efforts of the Vendome Parlor of the Native Daughters of the Golden West to be an historic monument to their pioneer forebears. Planned and executed over a period of three years, the cabin was formally dedicated on Sunday, September 24, 1916. Many locally prominent citizens were involved in the building of the cabin. The architects Theodore Lenzen and F.D. Wolf offered their services. Redwood logs were donated by Antone Matty of Wright's Station in the Santa Cruz mountains. Hours of volunteer labor went into the construction.

Originally planned to be placed on a hill where plantings were already set, it was later decided that the cabin should be built where it would be more accessible to the elderly. Only 30 by 32 feet, it is not clear what the cabin's function was to have been, except perhaps an occasional gathering place for the Native Daughters.

That Sunday afternoon 73 years ago was a festive one for the crowd that gathered at the park for the dedication. The Native Daughters and their friends were entertained by members of the locally famous Brohaska Orchestra (Tillie Brohaska was the past president of the Vendome Parlor), and Mr. Gene Cagney gave a rendition of "I Love You, California." Lorenzo Dow Stephens, a genuine pioneer, read one of his longer poems which drew parallels between the cabin and the world renowned Lick Observatory. Judge W.A. Beasley of the Superior Count gave an address summarizing the history of the state. He lauded the Native Daughters for their unselfish work.

Mrs. Mamie P. Carmichael, grand president of the Native Daughters of California, presented the pioneer memorial to the city with these words: *This simple and appropriate memorial that we have erect-* *ed in San Jose's playground will tend to unite the historic and romantic past with the prosaic and history making present and will strengthen California's treasured tradition and their hallowed influence for the benefit of future sons and daughters of the state."*

This symbolic gesture made long ago was not an isolated incident. In fact it was part of a great wave of concern, some might call it nostalgia, for our nation's recent past. The wilderness had been conquered, the frontier was no more and the westering days were over. These feelings were manifested in the founding of youth organizations such as the Boy Scouts and the Campfire Girls. There was considerable, if belated, interest in the American Indian. Pioneer societies across the country put up log cabin memorials in their parks. Perhaps the most notable of these which still remains is the one in Golden Gate Park.

The Landmarks Commission members felt that the Alum Rock log cabin qualified for official landmark status under four of the seven criteria:

(1) The cabin could be identified or associated with persons, eras, or events that have contributed to local history in a distinctive, significant way.

(2) It could be identified with a distinctive vestige of architectural style, design or method of construction.

(3) It could be associated with a master architect, builder, artist or craftsperson — in this case, Lenzen and Wolf.

(4) It provides for existing and future generations an example of the physical surroundings in which past generations lived and worked.

The current generation of Native Daughters renewed their interest in the cabin and initiated the papers for landmark status. This was recommended by the Commission, and the City Council approved the nomination on June 15, 1982.

On May 22, 1983, a gathering, not unlike the one held 67 years earlier, was held at the cabin to dedicate the bronze plaque supplied by the Vendome Parlor of the Native Daughters.

Once a memorial, always a memorial.

*East San Jose Fire Department, 1910.*
*San Jose Historical Museum Collections.*

# East San Jose: City of 2,000 Days

THE SHORT-LIVED CITY OF EAST SAN JOSE MAY HAVE been typical of a number of small towns that were destined to be swallowed up by San Jose, but its history is none-the-less unique. Originally incorporated in 1906 in a fever of prohibitionist sentiment, the little city surrendered, five years later, to the inevitable by voting to be annexed to San Jose.

The story is as follows:

The first signs of settlement east of Coyote Creek were in evidence in 1869 when A.T. Herrmann surveyed the first subdivision for the East San Jose Homestead Association. By 1876 *Thompson and West's Historical Atlas* of the county listed 250 residents. Soon the area was extended east to King Road with the addition of the Lendrum Tract and south to William Street with the Beach addition. The rural setting was ideal for Dr. Lewis Belknap's Garden City Sanitarium, one of the first such institutions to develop east of Coyote Creek.

The impetus for incorporation was brought about by the concern on the part of some of the more solid citizens over the number of saloons which seemed to be cropping up along Alum Rock Avenue. Under the loose supervision of the County Sheriff, the five saloons seemed inconsistent with the wholesome environment desired by such important locals as lumberman Frank H. Moon, builder C.A. Bates, attorney Jackson Hatch and print shop owner T.M. Wright. Wright, a God-fearing Presbyterian who took every opportunity to smite sin wherever he found it, spent sixteen years in the California Assembly where he authored the state's anti-liquor law known as the "little Volstead Act."

The forces opposed to incorporation were less visible but included the liquor interests and their supporters, the Knights of the Royal Arch, a local fraternal organization not opposed to lifting a glass or two in jolly fellowship. Their spokesman was well-known attorney John W. Sullivan.

At a meeting to discuss incorporation a number of issues were raised by the opposition, including the fear that rural mail service would be lost. Other opponents were concerned that they would be assessed for the building and maintenance of bridges across Coyote Creek.

Jackson Hatch quickly dispatched these concerns. On the issue of the Santa Clara Street Bridge he said: *The bridge is good for ten or fifteen years. It has not cost more at the utmost than two or three hundred dollars a year. The railroad is obliged to care for the part of it occupied by its tracks and two feet on either side. The rest of the expense is minute.* He further stated: *At common law there is no rule by which San Jose could compel East San Jose to pay one dollar to build a bridge*

*A.D.M. Cooper's Studio, c. 1910.*
*San Jose Historical Museum Collections.*

*which San Jose might need ... I think that if the time ever comes when it seems necessary to build a bridge the people of this community will have enough American enterprise to pay our just share.* (As it happened, the Santa Clara Street Bridge did collapse, eleven years later, under the weight of prune-laden boxcars.)

Also at the meeting was Arthur Free of Mountain View who was called upon to relate his city's successful experience of incorporation. Besides listing all the advantages of better roads and police and fire protection, he attempted to assuage the liquor interests by saying: *We have been able to regulate the saloon business ... the result that the income has increased and disorder almost disappeared. This has been accomplished without antagonizing the saloon men, as all saloonkeepers who are decent realize that certain restrictions are necessary.*

At a final meeting prior to the election on July 20, 1906, the *San Jose Mercury* reported that Hatch and Moon: *pledged themselves that they were not for the elimination, but for the regulation of the liquor traffic, and that in that attitude they would persist. They however named some resorts which they asserted should under present condition not exist.*

Perhaps these various assurances were enough to persuade the electorate, for when the votes were counted the drys and the incorporationists had won — by a majority of two votes. F.W. Moon became the Chairman of the new Board of Trustees which also included D.L. Schaaf, clerk; J.M. Robinson, recorder; John R. Cunan, treasurer; and Jackson Hatch, attorney. The *Mercury* article bannered: *Hatchets Buried When Fight Ends.*

As it turned out the hatchets were used on the saloonkeepers who were soon regulated right out of town. City ordinances 24 and 29 provided police regulation of places of indecent or immoral character and prohibited any individual or organization's owning, possessing, selling, distributing or giving away liquor. The taste in the mouths of the drinkers of East San

Jose must have been sour as well as dry as they reflected on all the pre-election talk of "moderation."

The newly incorporated city's boundaries were Coyote Creek on the west, King Road to the east, McKee Road to the north and William Street to the south. The newly appointed city fathers established the first volunteer fire department which was housed near the new City Hall at Santa Clara and Adams Street (now 23rd). This block also included the East San Jose School, the jail and the public library donated by Andrew Carnegie (see below). The citizens voted for $60,000 in sewer bonds to take care of the town's sanitary needs and to drain the continually flooded Lendrum district. Excess funds from these bonds went for new sidewalks and street repairs. In addition to the laws prohibiting liquor and saloons, there were ordinances prohibiting the placing of notices on trees, bridges or other town property or the erection of billboards. Weed abatement and proper trimming of trees and shrubs were also required by law. It was obvious that the good citizens of East San Jose wanted to show up the vice-ridden city across the creek.

Perhaps the little city's most noted resident was the renowned artist Astley David Middleton Cooper (1856-1924). A.D.M. Cooper came from a well-to-do family in Missouri. He traveled widely and had his works shown in Europe and the East. Famous for his scenes of American Indian life, he also painted classical and religious subjects. It is not known how his life size nudes, many of which were to be found in bars across the country, were accepted by his prudish neighbors. As a frequent habitué of the local saloons, Cooper couldn't have been too happy with the results of incorporation. His studio, built on San Antonio Street in 1909, became an instant landmark. Designed in a bizarre Egyptian style, it could easily have been confused with the Rosecrucian buildings later constructed at Park and Naglee. The studio is long gone, but the artist's Victorian cottage still stands at 250 South 19th Street.

After the spurt of civic improvement, the worthies of East San Jose seemed to tire of the efforts, all done without remuneration, of running a small town. As the *San Jose Mercury* put it: *feeling that it had accomplished what it started out to do, first to gain a "dry" town and a sewer system ... the burden of government was becoming more or less irksome and much might be gained if it were consolidated with San Jose.* Interest in consolidation coincided with

reforms in San Jose's formerly corrupt city government. The thought of their city being run by San Jose's new professional city manager system might have appealed to the east siders.

An excerpt of a letter written by a prominent citizen of East San Jose to the *Mercury* seemed to sum up the situation: *We come in feeling that we have accomplished a great deal over there the last five years, and that from now on our interest lies with 'Greater San Jose.' Our hardest fight is to overcome that loyalty to the little town which makes it hard for many of our citizens to pull down the flag. Give them a welcome when they come in. We have no axes to grind, and support no faction, but will try and make ourselves felt on the side of 'Better and Greater San Jose.'*

T.M. Wright and his former adversary John W. Sullivan, along with most of the members of the town council actively promoted the vote for annexation. Conspicuously absent was attorney Jackson Hatch who had been sentenced to prison in 1910 for embezzling funds from one of his clients.

Proponents did their work well, for when the votes were counted, the *Mercury's* morning edition of November 3, 1911 announced: *Consolidation Election Carried Yesterday by Overwhelming Vote.* Unlike the paltry two vote margin in 1906, the vote from East San Jose was ten to one for consolidation. San Jose residents voted five to one in favor of the measure.

And so East San Jose, the city of 2,000 days, passed into memory to become part of our greater San Jose history. A.D.M. Cooper and the boys of the Knights of the Royal Arch must have rejoiced at the prospect of once again lifting a glass in a neighborhood saloon.

## East San Jose Carnegie Library

A lasting tribute to the good citizens of the former City of East San Jose is the Carnegie Library at Santa Clara and 23rd Streets. It is one of the few library buildings endowed by industrialist Andrew Carnegie which still functions as a library for residents in the area. (San Jose's Carnegie Library ceased to function as such in 1937 and was razed in 1960.) The petite neo-classic structure, designed by noted local architect Jacob Lenzen, was completed in 1908 at a cost of $7,000. East San Jose City Attorney Jackson Hatch was the man most instrumental in bringing about the transaction.

The library was the center of local concern when the city proposed to raze it in the late 1970s. Irate

*East San Jose Carnegie Library, c. 1977.*
*San Jose Historical Museum Collections.*

citizens rose up under the leadership of Gordon Smelzer to form the Save the Carnegie Committee. After due consideration, the City decided that not only would the library stay, but that a $350,000 addition would be funded.

# The Smith House:
# An Evergreen Landmark

THE CITY OF SAN JOSE MUST HAVE SEEMED VERY far away when Francis Smith and his brother Charles purchased the land near the east foothills that would become the center of the little settlement of Evergreen. This property, which the Smiths acquired in 1867, was part of the original Spanish land grant of the Antonio Chaboya family, and was known as Rancho Yerba Buena. Some of the other families to settle on the Rancho property had names which are familiar as street names today: Hellyer, Cottle, Tully and Quimby.

The Smith brothers were Germans who emigrated from Hesse-Darmstadt to Schenectady, New York in 1861. While in New York, Francis learned the coopers trade, and also married Catherine Schiely, the daughter of another emigrant. Francis Smith arrived in Evergreen on Christmas Day 1867, and on May 15, 1868, he and his brother opened the first commercial establishment in the area, the Smith Brothers Store. Soon there would be a thriving blacksmith shop, and later, the first winery.

Francis, or Frank as he was known by his neighbors, became the Postmaster of Evergreen and traveled twice a week to San Jose to bring back the mail. Payment for this position was $12 per year. After the Wehner Vineyard and Winery were established in the 1890s, the mail deliveries were increased to three per week.

*Residence of Charles C. Smith and Store and Residence of Frank J. Smith, as pictured in the* Historical Atlas of Santa Clara County *by Thompson and West, 1876.*

The little store became Frank's exclusively when in the 1880s Charles sold his holdings and moved to San Jose to become a real estate developer. By then, the store had become the social center of Evergreen and Frank Smith became the settlement's titular mayor. During the brief quicksilver boom on what was to become Silver Creek, it was Frank Smith who staked and outfitted the prospectors and miners.

Many of the flights of Santa Clara County's pioneer aviator, John J. Montgomery, were made in Evergreen, and it was from the Smith store that the world heard of Professor Montgomery's fatal crash on October 31, 1911.

Frank Smith died in 1919, and the store he operated for 51 years burned in 1929.

As for the Smith House, Frank's daughter Kate remembered:

*Our house was built in 1874. It is solid redwood; the walls are not plastered even though they look like they are. Mother was here when the 1868 earthquake came and she lived above the store and held her arms on the walls as though to keep them from falling down. She said, 'if I ever build a house it will be all lumber.' Father had only $400 to invest in a house and this redwood house was built for that sum. It has ten rooms and never succumbed to earthquake tremors.*

Kate Smith, who lived in the house until her death at age 103 in 1973, had been one of the County's leading citizens. She was graduated from the rural Evergreen school (since turned into a church and now an apartment building), attended San Jose Normal and became a teacher. She taught in Evergreen School for four years and later taught 16 years at the old Grant School in downtown San Jose. Other teaching duties took her to Palo Alto and also to the Central Valley.

For many years she had the distinction of being San Jose State's oldest living graduate and rarely missed the annual Golden Grad luncheon at the College. Many of her pupils, some of whom rose to high places, returned often to extend their thanks to "Aunt Kate." The K.R. Smith School in Evergreen is named in her honor.

The Smith House stands today on a 4.7 acre lot surrounded by trees, near the corner of San Felipe and Fowler Roads, seemingly oblivious to the intense development arising on all sides. The house is begin-

ning to show the effects of time; the porch is decaying and woodpeckers have made rows of holes along the roofline. The tank house has completely crumbled and the privy is leaning precariously to the east.

The beauty of the house from a preservationist's point of view is that it still looks very much as it did when it was built. There have been only minor alterations since it was constructed in 1874 (compare the 1876 *Thompson and West* drawing with the current photo), and the surrounding acreage with its orchard and garden plot add to its rural charm.

With the rampant urbanization of the East Valley, such a peaceful place is a reminder to the new residents of what a unique settlement Evergreen was in its early years.

*The Frank J. Smith residence in Evergreen, as it appears today. Photo courtesy of Jack Douglas.*

*Summer Kitchen.*

# The William Wehner Estate

IGH ON A HILL OVERLOOKING THE VALLEY SITS the majestic Wehner mansion. Looking out through the century old trees, the old home seems to be brooding. Stripped of its vineyards, uncertain of its fate, it waits for the paltry efforts of today's men and women to decide if it will be allowed to co-exist with the ever expanding Villages retirement community.

In the 19th century when the estate was planned, giants like James Lick, Leland Stanford and James Phelan strode the land. Such a man was William Wehner who was described by Charles Sullivan in his book: *Like Modern Edens* as "the most important individual in regional winegrowing 1905-1915." Like many of the settlers in the Evergreen area, Wehner was a German immigrant. Unlike them, he had made his fortune prior to moving west. A talented artist with a keen business sense, he specialized in the creation of large painted panoramas which were installed in many prestigious buildings in the 1880s and 90s. Among the more celebrated of these was the *Crucifixion of Christ, The Battle of Gettysburg*, and *Missionary Ridge*. Examples of his work could be seen in cities throughout the Eastern United States and in pre-1906 San Francisco.

Listed as a farmer when he entered the United States from Hanover in 1860, Wehner would wait three decades before returning to the soil, but when he did, it was to be on a large scale. He had the vision and the money to recreate a vast winegrowing estate like those he had admired in his native Germany. The property which he chose was originally part of the Rancho Yerba Buena and was purchased from rancher John McCarty. It was on a western slope and fed by active springs. Under the expert guidance of his brother Ernest, over 300 acres were planted with 175 imported grape varieties, all on resistant root stock. In addition they also planted over 5,000 fruit trees, including apricots, nectarines, peaches, French prunes, pears and olives.

Wehner called his estate Loma Azules and the winery the Highland Vineyards. Unlike most of the smaller vineyard owners who shipped their bulk product to San Francisco, Wehner produced premium wines under his own estate label. Known as a perfectionist, he may well have had the first scientifically planned and produced operation in the West. He per-

fected the process of cool fermentation of white wine, and as a result, his sauternes were rated as the finest in California. They continued to receive the highest evaluations nationwide for a quarter of a century.

A man of wealth and culture whose interests kept him away from the ranch a great deal, Wehner, never-the-less, spared no expense in making himself a comfortable country home. He hired the prestigious Chicago firm of Burnham and Root to design his hillside mansion in 1888. To this firm's credit were such landmark buildings as the Monadnock and Rookery buildings in Chicago, the Flatiron building in New York, the old Chronicle building and the Mills buildings in San Francisco and the Union Station in Washington D.C. The firm did few residential commissions, so their design for the Wehner Ranch is the only known example in California. The famous San Francisco architect Willis Polk began his career in the West as head of the San Francisco office of Burnham

*Wehner Residence. All photos by Romney Maupin.*

and Root, and as he was the architect of many of the homes of San Francisco's elite, he may well have been the principal designer of the Wehner mansion.

The three story mansion is built in a late Queen Anne style. The dominant feature is the repeated use of the round arch in the carriage entrance, doorways and porch windows. It had eight fireplaces and three bathrooms (two more were added later). The enclosed sunporch has a balcony above which leads out from the master bedroom. The house sits on a concrete and stone foundation and has a full basement below grade. Completed in 1891, it was built at a cost of $20,000.

Some of the mansion's most charming aspects are the outbuildings and the landscaping. The summer kitchen has many characteristics of the main house, including arched entryways, steeply pitched roof line and the patterned wood shingles. The small garden house, with its oversized fireplace, distinctive bullseye windows and overgrown patio must have been a cool comfortable summer retreat for the men with their cigars. Within the drive that circles the house are lawns and a network of brick paths. The many mature trees include palms, magnolias, fir and a giant monkey pod.

As magnificent as the house and grounds are, the most significant features historically are the many outbuildings from the 100 year old winery operation. These include the distinctive 1890 hillside winery building which utilized the force of gravity to move the crushed product to the fermenting tanks. This building and the adjacent barns are in extremely fragile condition. The larger 1908 winery building which is made of stone and redwood is, however, still functional and is presently being used to cellar wines from the nearby Mirassou Winery. Taken all together, the buildings on the Wehner Ranch are a complete historical exhibit of a 19th century estate winery, and as such they belong on the National Register of Historic Places.

But by 1915 the aging Wehner had sold a large portion of the estate to Albert Haentze, another experienced German winemaker and businessman from Chicago. Renaming the winery the Rancho Villa Vista, Haentze succeeded Wehner as leader of the Santa Clara Valley grape growers, but he fought a losing battle with the forces of prohibition which closed most wineries in 1918. When prohibition was lifted in 1933, the estate came under the control of the Cribari family who maintained the winery on the

1890 Winery.

site until 1959 when the land passed through the hands of several would-be developers. At one point in the early 60s it was considered as a possible site for the UC campus that was later built in Santa Cruz. Eventually it became the site for the Villages.

William Wehner was a leader in the development of the wine industry in California and in the promotion of the valley's wine. His good business sense and scientific management allowed him to weather the economic crisis of the 1890s, and the grapevine blight (phylloxera) that followed. During the great wine wars of the 1890s, Wehner was a leader of one of the rival wine cooperatives, the California Wine Corporation. By 1901 when most of the valley's smaller operations were on the verge of bankruptcy, Wehner produced 200,000 gallons of wine while making plans for an even bigger operation.

The Wehner estate is an extraordinary cultural resource, and, if developed, could be an asset to the community similar to that of the Villa Montalvo above Saratoga. Preserving the mansion and sharing its splendor and vitacultural history with the community will require the same daring and imagination that William Wehner had when he created his estate. Are there still such people in our age?

*Charles LeFranc*

# The Historic Almaden Winery

RECENT NEWSPAPER ARTICLES DECRY THE LOSS OF the Paul Masson Winery and a possible end to the 20 year tradition of "Music in the Vineyards." Very little has been written, however, about the departure of the Almaden Winery to San Benito County in 1987.

Historically the Masson operation pales in comparison to that of the Almaden Winery, located at 1530 Blossom Hill Road, which can claim the distinction of being the oldest in northern California.

Almaden Vineyards can trace its beginning back to the gold rush when Etienne Thée, a Bordeaux farmer, settled in the Santa Clara Valley. After some success at making wine from his vineyard of indigenous "mission" grapes, he went into partnership with Charles Le Franc, a tailor from Passy, France whom he met in the expanding French community of San Jose. Unhappy with the quality of the wine made from local grapes, Le Franc was the first winemaker in northern California to import European stock (vitis vinifera) to produce the varietal wines familiar today. These early cuttings, Pinot, Sauvignon, Semillon, Cabernet and Grenache, were grafted onto the mission root stock.

Le Franc married Thée's daughter Marie Adele in 1857 and became the proprietor of the Almaden "Sweet Grape Vineyard." He soon added to his holdings by purchasing an adjacent vineyard for $250. A shrewd businessman, Le Franc realized that there was a growing market for quality wines and brandies in California, and he set in motion a company that would eventually be the third largest producer of varietal wines in the nation. By 1862 the Almaden Vineyard consisted of 75 acres producing approximately 100,000 gallons of varietal wine which was winning prizes at county fairs and competitions. Le Franc represented the county at the first California Wine Convention in San Francisco in 1862.

In 1869 Le Franc added some German varietals to his stock by transplanting Johannesburg Riesling and Traminer vines from a vineyard owned by Frank Stock which had been located at Eighth and William Streets. Le Franc used innovative vitacultural practices such as setting vines on close centers to increase the intensity of the flavors. His ports and angelicas were known for their longevity, and his Malbec vines were the only large acreage of fine Bordeaux vines in the West.

During the depression of the 1870s the Almaden Winery thrived while others in the Valley went broke. 1876 saw the expansion of the winery and the addition of the substantial sandstone winery building. Le Franc sent a ten foot high carved cask of his wine (capacity 3,447 gallons) to the nation's centennial in Philadelphia that year. (The same barrel returned for the bi-centennial of 1976.)

The devastating epidemic of phylloxera in France was advantageous to Le Franc, for not only did it diminish imports of French wine thereby opening new markets for the California product, but it convinced a young Frenchman named Paul Masson to seek his fortune in San Jose.

Masson, who originally came to San Jose to study business at the University of the Pacific, became friends with Le Franc and his family which included the three children Henry, Louise and Marie. Masson returned to France briefly before returning to help market Almaden Wines for Le Franc. It was while working for Almaden that the young Masson began experimenting with sparkling wines, eventually setting up his champagne cellars. Masson first worked out of Almaden's business outlet at 163-169 West Santa Clara Street (the building which is now occupied by the D.B. Cooper Saloon) until he established his own outlet on East Santa Clara Street.

Charles Le Franc continued to be a leader in the California wine industry until his tragic death in October, 1887 when he was trampled while attempting to stop a team of runaway horses. His son Henry quickly assumed control of the business. Paul Masson, shortly afterward, married Louise Le Franc and became part of the family. Masson, absorbed in

The Almaden Vineyards in 1891.

his own champagne operation, probably did not guess that someday he would control the combined family fortune, but that is just what happened when Henry Le Franc and his wife Louise Delmas Le Franc were killed when an inter-urban trolley smashed into their car on a county road. Their daughter Nelty, thrown from the car, survived.

Masson managed both enterprises right up to and into Prohibition. While most wineries went out of business during this period, the crafty Masson sold his grapes for juice and also became certified to produce sacramental and medicinal wines. The aging winemaker sold the operation to the Almaden Vineyard Corporation, headed by Charles M. Jones, in 1930.

When Prohibition was lifted in 1933, Jones, who had a large inventory of wine stockpiled by Masson, was ready for full production. As one might guess, a whole lot of inferior wine was quickly produced by start-up wineries. Jones, as a founder and first director of the Wine Institute, did much to establish standards to improve the quality of California wines.

After Jones's death in 1940 the Almaden winery was purchased by Louis Benoist and Brayton Wilbur. These San Francisco businessmen revitalized much of the vineyard stock and began purchasing vineyards beyond Santa Clara County. Benoist, who appreciated Almaden's traditions, had the old Le Franc ranch house restored in a French Victorian manner. He hired the former Novitiate brother and winemaker Oliver Goulet to create many distinguished wines. Goulet's Grenache Rosé, with clever marketing, changed the nation's drinking habits.

Another important member of the new team was Frank Schoonmaker, a connoisseur and wine author. Schoonmaker enlisted the viticulturists of the University of California in experimenting with grape varieties in areas of Monterey and San Benito counties. Almaden started the movement that led to the area becoming one of the largest wine producing regions of the world. During the 1940s and 50s Almaden won top awards for many of its wines and helped to make California wines serious competitors to the European imports.

In 1967, at the height of its success, Louis Benoist sold the winery to National Distillers. During their stewardship Almaden rose to become the third largest wine producer in the U.S., and by 1980 the largest producer of premium varietal wines. Thus,

*Paul Masson. Photo from* A Centennial History of the Sainte Claire Club 1888-1988.

Charles Le Franc's vision of making good, inexpensive, varietal wines available to all was fulfilled.

During this last period the management turned the historic property into a showplace. They built a lavish chateau-style structure to house their offices, and they installed a helicopter pad to facilitate quick trips to the airport and San Francisco. A magnificent rose garden, named for Louis Benoist, was planted, and the original 1850 winery building was remodeled for wine tasting and sales. Unfortunately the original Le Franc ranch house burned to the ground in the mid-1970s.

All of this interest in the historic property ceased when National Distillers became part of the giant Heublein liquor cartel. Heublein chose to consolidate their interests by moving the winemaking and bottling operations closer to the source of their grapes. While this made good economic sense, it sounded the death knell to the last of Santa Clara County's great agricultural traditions.

**Note:** On June 2, 1989 workers dismantling the modern structures to make way for a planned housing development accidentally set fire to the buildings. The historic sandstone winery building went up in flames as well as the antique wine cask that had been displayed in Philadelphia at the nation's centennial, 1876 and bicentennial, 1976.

Hotel Sainte Claire at San Jose, California, in The Valley of Heart's Delight.
Postcard courtesy of Jack Douglas.

# The Sainte Claire Hotel

THE SECOND GRAND RE-OPENING OF THE SAINTE CLAIRE Hotel in Spring 1992 offered us an opportunity to reflect on the history of this queen of San Jose's hostelries. When it was built in 1926 it figured in real estate mogul T.S. Montgomery's master plan for San Jose much as the recent Fairmont Hotel does to our current redevelopment plans. It was to be Montgomery's crown jewel of his downtown empire and a focal point for the growing city's social and cultural life. Also, it was to be followed by a new civic auditorium that would serve as a convention center. Montgomery's death and the Great Depression postponed the auditorium until 1934.

The mid-1920s saw a veritable boom in construction in downtown San Jose. In addition to the Sainte Claire there were the Trinkler Dohrmann, Medico Dental, Bank of Italy, Commercial and Knights of Columbus buildings and the California Theatre.

There were substantial additions to the YWCA, Burrell, Ryland and Garden City Bank buildings as well. Many of these projects were backed by Montgomery and his Mercantile Trust Company.

In 1923 Montgomery purchased the 70 year old Eagle Brewery at the corner of San Carlos and Market Streets for the site of his new hotel. The Eagle, along with all the nation's breweries, had been closed by Prohibition in 1918. Montgomery, who had made his fortune in local land speculation, used the system that had worked successfully in developing his other South First Street enterprises. On the premise that the new hotel would raise their property values, he appealed to investors who already had holdings in the immediate area. Within weeks he had a hundred prominent stock subscribers, including: Hi Baggerly *(San Jose News)*, F.L. Burrell, the Borcher Brothers, Fred Doerr, The Hales, W.C. Lean, G.E.

Lenzen, Ernest Lion, Jay McCabe, Charles O'Brien, E.H. Renzel, John Twohy, Walter Trinkler, Charles P. Weeks and W.P. Day. The last two of these comprised the firm of Weeks and Day, noted San Francisco architects who were to design the new hotel.

It is indicative of the importance of the Sainte Claire to Montgomery that he reached beyond his local architectural firm, Binder and Curtis, to bring in Weeks and Day. They were also, at the time, preparing plans for the Mark Hopkins Hotel on Nob Hill. Similarities between the two hotels are quite apparent. Other major commissions done by this firm included the State Library, the State Building (now called the Jesse Unruh Building), the Fox Oakland Theatre and our own California Fox Theatre.

Ground breaking took place on September 10, 1925, and the hotel was completed by late September the following year. Cahill Brothers of San Francisco did the construction work at a cost of approximately $750,000. The equipment and furnishings brought the price tag to an even million. Robinson and Sons Furniture at First and San Carlos won the contract to provide the custom built furnishings. The antique lobby furnishings came from Czechoslovakia.

The management of the Sainte Claire was leased to the nationally known firm of hotel operators, J.A. and S.J. Newcomb, for 20 years at $1,500,000. William A. Newcomb, son of the the former, moved to San Jose to personally manage the hotel. Most of the supervisory staff came from hotels across the country — several had European backgrounds.

The Sainte Claire was the first major hotel to be built in San Jose since the Montgomery Hotel was built at First and San Antonio in 1911, and it far exceeded it in overall space and lavishness. The biggest and best hotel between San Francisco and Los Angeles, its six stories included 200 beautifully furnished guest rooms, 22 sales sample rooms, several residential suites, a ballroom, restaurant, coffee shop and dining room, as well as several street level shops. The luxurious lounge (no liquor until 1933) featured ornate antique furnishings, hand-painted beam ceilings and an impressive fireplace. A unique feature was the enclosed Spanish courtyard with its striking tile fountain which was custom-made by Albert Solon, the internationally known ceramicist who had a tile factory here in San Jose.

At the completion celebration banquet for the stockholders, T.S. Montgomery praised his fellow business partners: *We are friends to each other, if we were not friends there would be no Sainte Claire. I called on 95% of the stockholders personally and they*

Postcard of El Patio courtesy of Jack Douglas.

*came through nobly. ... A promoter offered to raise the money for $40,000 but I told him,'I know a bunch that will do it for 40 cents.' He said, 'It can't be done.' I replied, ' it will be done.' Behold your achievement.*

The new hotel was opened with great fanfare on October 16, 1926 with a black tie party for 500. In the next day's *Mercury Herald*, Margaret Craven, society editor, wrote: *Five hundred people, all dressed up in their best bib and tucker, found out last night that the bigger San Jose we all dream about is just around the corner knocking to be let in. They suspicioned it when they saw the doorman — looking as if he had stepped out of a Cecil DeMille film — in a brand new blue suit with a row of brand new brass buttons and a face like a cigar store Indian.*

*They anticipated it when they pushed their way through the swinging doors into the lobby of the new Hotel Sainte Claire and Oh'd and My'd at the hand-painted ceiling, the antique walnut and the Czecho-Slovakian chairs.*

*But it wasn't until they were safely seated in the dining room and had put their teeth into something or other that had a French name, and looked about them and saw all their neighbors and their best friends, and the men they owed money to and from whom they* had bought their cars, that they knew, realized and could swear to it that they were in San Jose, and not in some eastern hostelry or a famous resort pictured in each month's *Vanity Fair.*

By the next day many felt that San Jose had risen above its "prune town" image and might one day rival San Francisco for sophistication and elegance. The local Kiwanis, Lions, Soroptimists and Optimists immediately signed on to schedule their luncheon meetings, and weddings, proms and other special events were soon crowding the hotel's calendar. The opening of the upstart De Anza Hotel in 1931 barely made a ripple in the Sainte Claire's reputation as San Jose's premier hotel.

Had we not abandoned downtown for the suburbs, the Sainte Claire might have maintained this position, but as business declined so did the hotel. By the 1970s it had reached the nadir of its existence as a low income residence facility.

In 1980, with the redevelopment of downtown underway and a new convention center being planned, local developer Stephen Lin purchased the hotel, restored the lower public areas and opened it under the Hilton banner.

He then sold it to an investment company which

*Pictured is the restored Palm Room lounge in the recently reopened Hotel Sainte Claire.*

planned to continue the renovation. They failed in this effort, and after a period during which it was in receivership, the hotel was acquired by the Mobedshahi Group which has gone to great lengths to bring the rooms up to modern day standards.

Fortunately they were equally concerned with restoring much of the historic fabric of the hotel and the revealing of many of the features that were painted over or covered by years of "modernization." The Spanish courtyard, covered over in the 1950s, has been painstakingly reconstructed so that natural light may stream once again through the oval windows in the lounge, lobby and restaurant areas. The Sainte Claire is open again, and a new generation can marvel at the quality of this fine old building.

# New Life For The Medico-Dental Building

THE 1920s HIGHRISE MEDICO-DENTAL BUILDING at the corner of West Santa Clara and Sixth Streets has been renovated and put to new use as highrise condominiums by the Aspen West Corporation. The building has had an important place in the recent history of our city, and with its many outstanding architectural features is a prime candidate for placement on the National Register of Historic Places. It is a registered city landmark.

Opened on April 7, 1928, the building was the result of the vision of a group of doctors and dentists to provide a one-stop medical facility for the city's growing population. These professionals recognized that medical services were subject to the same merchandising concepts as other products and that

Photos by Romney Maupin.

patients could be influenced in their choice of a doctor by the convenience of a concentrated collective medical operation. This new phenomenon also reflected the growing importance of the automobile, for the adjacent parking facility was a major feature of such a structure. Similar buildings arose in other cities to accomplish this objective. For example, the beautiful Art Deco building at 450 Sutter in San Francisco with its enormous subterranean garage was finished in 1930, and still functions as a center for many of that city's medical professionals.

Our own Medico-Dental Building, modest by San Francisco standards, was one of four skyscrapers built in San Jose prior to the crash of 1929. Designed by the distinguished California architect William Weeks, the Medico-Dental Building was the most up-to-date facility of its kind when it opened in 1928.

Weeks started his career as a designer of Victorian-style homes in Watsonville, then went on to design many schools, libraries, public buildings and hotels throughout California. His Spanish motif Art Deco Palomar Hotel in Santa Cruz has many similarities to the Medico-Dental Building and also to our De Anza Hotel. The De Anza, however, was designed by his son H.H. Weeks.

These buildings are all reinforced concrete structures, highlighted by strong vertical lines and numerous decorative features. The Medico-Dental Building is by far the strongest statement of the three and as it was built during the affluent 1920s, has the most expensive detailing. Such features as the lavish terra cotta keystone entryway with its hand stenciled ceilings and marble walls would grace any cathedral (as reported in the *Mercury Herald.)* The building rises to a full ten stories, with an eleventh floor set back to allow access to roof gardens on the east and west. This floor, which houses a large public room, is crowned with terra cotta shields and torches. A giant winged figure stands in the center. Presumably the angel of mercy, it clasps the medical caduceus to its breast. The toga-clad figure wears a curious warlike spartan helmet, the origins of which are unknown. (No, I don't think Weeks had the San Jose State Spartans in mind when he selected the figure).

---

Prior to the opening of the Medico-Dental Building, San Joseans visited their doctors and dentists in the second and third floor offices of buildings along First and Second Streets. An old photo of the Bank of Italy shows a large sign above the bank advertising the services of "Painless Parker," dentist. The Twohy Building, the 1917 five story structure at First and San Antonio (now regrettably renamed the "Paseo" Building) was the home of many of the medical professionals who banded together to form the Medico-Dental company which sold shares to the public and to the professionals who were to have offices in the new building. Each dentist or doctor who had stock was allowed to design the plan of his own office which made for a variety of layouts and decor. A photo in the *Mercury Herald* of a young woman sitting in one of the new waiting rooms exclaims: *Luxurious furniture makes waiting a pleasure.*

Practically the whole issue of the Saturday morning edition of the April 7th *Mercury Herald* was taken up with news and congratulatory advertising of the opening of San Jose's new one-stop medical service. The first two floors housed medical services, including, on first floor, a pharmacy with a lunch counter. The San Jose Clinical Laboratory and Bischoff's Surgical Supply occupied the second floor. This floor also included Winton and Palmer's Beauty Parlor and a barber shop. Tutt and Puterbough operated a prosthetic service on the eighth floor. The garage in the back provided parking and a full service filling station. Patients who previously had to walk or take a streetcar to downtown, and in many cases climb several flights of stairs, could now drive to the rear entrance where in a few short steps, they could be wafted by elevator to the upper floors.

My own personal memories of the building were as a patient of Dr. Gerald B. Myers who had an office on the tenth floor. (Dentists got most of the north and east exposures so as to have more even natural light.) On a clear day, between drillings and spittings, I could see north as far

as the Bay Bridge. Dr. Myers, one of the original tenants, was the last professional in the building when he retired in the mid-1970s.

One of the extra features of the building was the eleventh floor ballroom. This large room had a generous fireplace and high ceilings with hand-stenciled crossbeams. French doors led out to the roof garden from which one could (and still can) have an unobstructed view in all directions. The *Mercury Herald* reporter Eric Johnston waxed poetical as he described the scene in 1928: *From this point of vantage (the roof garden) one has a superb view of the entire valley. Below lie the city streets spreading away to the fields and orchards. These melt into the hills, rising at this season of the year green and rose and purple. Standing in the Roof Garden, one reflects that the spot is well named "Valley of the Heart's Delight."*

According to Dr. Myers, the ballroom never became the popular public room that the builders had in mind. Perhaps the depression or the competition from the soon to be built De Anza eclipsed this attractive feature. Or did the locals find it hard to imagine having fun in a building that was sometimes associated with pain?

The Medico-Dental Building functioned as the city's central medical office building up until the

*Angel of Mercy atop the Medico-Dental Building.*

1950s when the exodus from downtown to the suburbs took place. In the early 1970s the building was renovated for conventional offices and the name was changed to "Vintage Towers."

When the Aspen Corporation rehabilitated the building for condominiums, it once again became a vital part of the downtown scene. For many old timers like myself, it will always be associated with trips to the dentist, or the place where we lost our appendix, or the many malts and grilled cheese sandwiches consumed at the pharmacy lunch counter. It will go down in the history books, however, as a symbol of a revolutionary new concept of doctor-patient care brought about by such technological innovations as the highrise elevator and the automobile.

# The De Anza Hotel

*Pamphlet cover of De Anza Hotel courtesy of Jack Douglas.*

THE MOST SIGNIFICANT EVENT in the 1990 downtown San Jose redevelopment was the grand opening, in November, of the restored De Anza Hotel. This Moderne (art deco) style skyscraper was a major addition to the city skyline when it was constructed sixty years ago, and although it has become somewhat dwarfed by more recent highrises, its unique style and position on West Santa Clara Street assures that it will remain a major City landmark.

Much of San Jose's recent history is associated with this gem of a building. From the 1930s to the 1960s almost everyone, at one time or another, attended meetings, parties, dances and weddings there. Some of our finest food and entertainment was offered, along with such services as barber shops, beauty parlors and travel agencies.

The conception and financing of the hotel was an interesting story in itself. During the palmy days of the 1920s the smaller cities which couldn't attract big investors to build hotels came up with the idea of forming a corporation and selling shares to local citizens in order to construct a hotel building which would then be leased to a professional hotel operator. Included in the strategy was the rule that only local contractors and supplies would be used. This insured that everyone down to the lowliest laborer

De Anza Lounge 1940.

had a personal stake in the success of the project. In the case of the De Anza this became a critical factor, for shortly after the money was raised, the stock market crash of October 1929 sent the nation into the Great Depression.

The hotel corporation was headed by Alex Hart whose department store would be in the shadow of the new hotel. Many other West Santa Clara Street businessmen were large investors, including real estate man W.S. Clayton, auto dealers Fritz Campen and Louis Normandin, and *Mercury* publisher Everis Hayes. Several contractors who worked on the building, such as Carl Swenson, Fred Doerr and William Serpa were also shareholders.

The ground breaking ceremony for the new ten story $500,000 Hotel San Jose took place at 9:30 on the morning of February 26, 1930. The site at Santa Clara and Notre Dame Streets had stood empty since the Sisters of Notre Dame moved their college and

convent to Belmont's Ralston Estate in 1925. Carl N. Swenson had the winning low bid of $161,500 to become the general contractor.

The architectural firm of William Weeks was selected to design the building. Harold Weeks, son of the founder, did the final design. It had much in common with that of the firm's Medico Dental building which had been erected two years earlier on East Santa Clara Street. Both buildings have the same vertical lines, similar stylized Spanish and art deco ornamentation and similar height. Each building touted exterior windows in every room for ventilation and views. Both are topped with set-back penthouses with rooftop decks.

The Spanish Colonial motif was carried throughout the hotel in the form of stenciled beam ceilings and ornate balconies in the lobby and other public spaces. The furniture, all purchased from L. Lion and Son at Second and San Fernando, was designed specifically for the hotel. The corporation leaders must have been caught up in the enthusiasm for things Spanish, for not long before the opening the prosaically named Hotel San Jose became the Hotel De Anza. De Anza, said the *Mercury*, was "the first explorer to appreciate the possibilities of the Santa Clara Valley."

The De Anza Hotel opened its doors for the first time on February 26, 1931 under the management of Will R. Conway who had interests in several other hotels around the state. The first guest to sign the register was Hortense Lion, a younger member of the furniture family.

Billed as San Jose's "newest high rise fire-proof hotel," the De Anza had 135 sleeping rooms — all with bath, ten sample rooms for salesmen, a lounge, coffee shop and a banquet room off the mezzanine. When Prohibition was lifted in 1933, the hotel responded by adding, in the words of a *Mercury* reporter: *a unique new tap room, different than anything of its kind on the coast...in every detail it is modern, from the pressed wood floor to a flesh-colored lounge mirror. The latter is the only one of its kind on the coast, the original being shown at the World's Fair in Chicago last year. Another creation, patterned after the color tower at the Fair, is a rhododendron in a corner of the lounge which is made entirely of copper and has eight blossoms, all electrically lighted.*

The Will Conway regime was not all flowers, however. The management had gotten into consider-

*Inviting Club De Anza Tap Room 1940.*

able debt and was also being brought before the grand jury on a charge of bribing an official to fix a liquor license. It came as no surprise when Conway sold the lease in 1936 to San Francisco hotel tycoon Harry Richmond. Richmond appointed his two sons-in-law Maurice Metcalf and Thomas Fisher joint managers. They and their families moved to San Jose and soon became known throughout the community.

The De Anza came into its own in the late thirties and particularly during the war years when it was the hangout for GI's on leave. The sharper image of the De Anza appealed more to young people than did the more conservative Sainte Claire.

It was at the beginning of the Metcalf and Fisher management that Hilda Keast began her 25 year service at the hotel. She worked her way up to become hostess and arranger of the various meetings and social events. According to her daughter Dorothy Anderson, Mrs. Keast had her hands full during the war years when staffing was short and service men's families were sleeping on cots in the hallways. There was also the problem of keeping the hotel from becoming a glorified bordello full of GI's and their pickup girlfriends.

A number of celebrities stayed at the De Anza during this period. Eddie Bruce, a former bellhop, reminisced in the *Mercury* about the teenaged Mickey

Rooney running amok in the elevators and about delivering drinks to Susan Hayward, Fred MacMurray and Paulette Goddard. Eddie's big moment was getting Eleanor Roosevelt's autograph during one of her visits to the hotel.

A young woman named Shirlie Montgomery, later to become one of San Jose's most prominent photographers, got her start when the hotel staff photographer went off to war. Many a local young lady had her picture taken with servicemen in the Tahitian "Danzabar" by Ms. Montgomery.

San Jose continued to boom during the postwar years as many of the servicemen who had passed through during the war came back to settle in the area. The hotel management changed in 1950 (the original local owners had sold the building to the Handlery chain in 1942) and it was now taken over by Dean Ireland. His son William became resident manager. Many changes were made, including the rechristening of all the public rooms with Spanish names. The bar became El Capitan, the banquet room El Conquistador, the Flamingo Room the El Pajaro and the Danzabar became La Cantina. In 1957 the L-shaped pool would be a first for a major San Jose hotel, and the much discussed diving lady was emblazoned on the west wall of the building.

The Ireland's moved on in the late fifties and the hotel, like downtown itself, began a long slide to dete-

*Historic Hedley Club lounge in the restored De Anza Hotel.*

rioration. Used in the early seventies to house low income tenants, it was later condemned as a fire hazard. Several attempts to restore the building came to naught until the current developers, Saratoga Capital, with support from the Redevelopment Agency, put the building back on the track.

The interior of the DeAnza had been gutted by one of the previous developers, so the new owners had to totally redesign the inside. The one exception is the Hedley Lounge which still has its giant fireplace and quaint balconies. The designers have done an excellent job of recreating the Spanish Moderne atmosphere of the original, and there is a feeling of quality throughout the hotel. The first class restaurant, and the music and dancing in the lounge help to make the DeAnza Hotel, once again, a destination for travelers and local people as well.

# Down to the Station

Passenger Train at San Jose Station c. 1890. Market Street. San Jose Historical Museum Collections.

THERE WAS AN AIR OF EXCITEMENT ON JUNE 27, 1993 when the crowd gathered for the official opening of the city's new Tamien Station near Alma Street. A kilted bagpiper heralded the approach of CalTrain's first regular commuter special to Gilroy as the assembled railroad fans, politicians and curious citizens cheered. Riding in the engineer's cab was County Supervisor and transit tzar Rod Diridon who was decked out in unusually fresh-looking trainman togs.

The Tamien Station, surrounded by a vast parking lot, is the city's only link between light rail county transit and heavy rail CalTrain and Amtrak. The parallel platforms allow commuters to transfer from points south to light rail and also make it convenient for those on the light rail line to reach the CalTrain for trips up the Peninsula.

The numerous speakers on that June day, representing every branch of government involved in the creation of the station, all made reference to the beginning of a "new era" in public transit and to the day when Californians would be abandoning their cars for the convenience of train transit. Although it has seemed like forever (some were no doubt thinking), we are, at last, seeing some tangible results from our transit tax dollars.

The old Cahill Station has been the City's main terminal since it was dedicated on December 30, 1935. The construction of that station was the capstone of a major overhaul of San Jose's rail system that brought us into the 20th century of train travel.

A little background may be helpful in order to understand the importance of the railroad in early San Jose. The state of California was still in its infancy when the San Francisco and San Jose Railroad was completed in January 1864. A huge wooden shed on Bassett Street served as the main train station. Four years later the line was extended down Fourth Street south to Gilroy. In 1877 the narrow gauge South Pacific Railroad coursed through San Jose on its route from Alameda in the East Bay to Santa Cruz. It had a station at the spot where the Cahill Station now stands.

To those who had been limited to horse drawn vehicles, it must have seemed like a miracle to be whisked off to San Francisco, Oakland or Santa Cruz in two hour's time. Each new spur was looked upon as a symbol of progress in those early years.

When the Fourth Street line was put down, J.J. Owen, editor of the *Mercury* observed: *It is pleasing to behold one of our most undulating, muddiest and filthiest thoroughfares being transformed into a neat and tidy street ... Washington Square, we are informed, is to be plowed and on either side of the fence poplar trees are to be planted, thus adding beauty and in the future a shady retreat from the busy marts of our city.* The Fourth Street station was built between San Carlos and San Salvador for the convenience of students commuting to the recently constructed State Normal School (now San Jose State University).

But "progress" is never to be denied. At the turn of the century the automobile was beginning to make an appearance on our streets. Long waits for passing freight trains as they lumbered through downtown began to become an annoyance. By 1920 they were an outrage. One long train on Fourth Street could block every east-west street in all of downtown. The railroad that had brought early improvements to the east side of town was now responsible for detracting from the ambience of the elite Naglee Park neighborhood.

The railroad, by now controlled by Southern Pacific, had a franchise to operate on Fourth Street until 1916, and they intended to maintain the status quo as long past that date as possible. Southern Pacific's influence in San Jose ran very deep. Several of the most powerful people in town were on their payroll, including Louis Oneal who was their legal representative, and members of the Clayton family, owners of the First National Bank and the county's largest real estate firm, who handled all the railroad's local business. Influence from such as these was enough to defeat a 1923 bond issue to pay the city's share of the costs to build underpasses. In April 1925 SP, with the support of the Clayton controlled Chamber of Commerce and Merchant's Association petitioned the city to renew the Fourth Street franchise. To their credit, the City Council chose not to extend the franchise.

After several years of negotiations the SP finally gave in to re-routing their line to the west side of town where they owned some of the right-of-way. The big expense was not the new station or cost of the land, but the numerous overpasses and underpasses that would allow trains a free flow through the heart of town. The Cahill Station, the viaduct on West San Carlos and the underpass on The Alameda near Stockton were major construction jobs, not unwelcome in the depths of the depression. The cost of the entire project was $3.5 million, $1 million of which was allotted for the station.

The unincorporated district of Willow Glen was, perhaps, the most formidable obstacle to the new rail line. Owners of cozy new homes, including those in the exclusive Palm Haven development, weren't happy about their suburb being cut in two by a rail line. They voted to incorporate as a city so that they could reject any franchise that would allow the railroad in. A three year lawsuit went all the way to the Supreme Court where it was dismissed on procedural grounds. By this time the SP had purchased land which allowed it to skirt around Willow Glen.

San Jose's new Cahill Station brought all of the city's passenger service together under one roof. The street and station were named after Hiram Cahill, the pioneer rancher who once lived on the site. The building, designed by architect J. H. Christie and constructed by the Carl N. Swenson Company, was similar to those built by SP for Sacramento and Fresno. Characteristic were the subways under the tracks to the platforms. Although not as grand as the big city stations in the east, Cahill's cathedral ceilings, windows, enormous mural and solid brick construction reminded passengers that this was San Jose's temple to the god (SP) of transportation.

SP's god personified was President Angus McDonald. Once his attention was drawn to it he took a personal interest in ramrodding the San Jose project through to its conclusion. A frequent visitor to the site, he promised that they would complete the job by December 31, 1935, and true to his word, the trains were running by December 30th.

The last train to travel down Fourth Street on that December day, loaded with SP brass and other celebrants, headed south to make a curve beyond Oak Hill Cemetery and effect a triumphal approach to the new station where thousands were gathered to witness the dedication. City Council president Charles Bishop presided. Rev. L.C. Rudolph, President of the University of Santa Clara read the invocation and Angus McDonald gave the major address. There were several songs by the Amigos Club Quartet, and the SP band played the national anthem. Afterwards the West Santa Clara Street Development Association and its president Alex Hart hosted a lunch for the SP officials at the new De Anza Hotel. The association hoped that the railroad would improve business in their area, and indeed the De Anza did become the preferred hotel for traveling salesmen who arrived by train.

The opening of the new west side rail line freed San Jose of 70 years of rail crossing tie-ups and cleared the way for automobile traffic. Now, of course, it is the automobile that is helping to destroy the quality of life in the Santa Clara Valley. Many hope that a new rail system, with hubs like the Tamien Station, will be the people movers of the future. Let us pray that they are right.

*Southern Pacific Depot c. 1940. Cahill and San Fernando Streets. Photo from* Prune County Railroading *by Holmes.*

# Where is Washington Square?

EW OLD TIME RESIDENTS CAN TELL YOU WHERE TO find San Jose's Washington Square. Lost for several generations on the San Jose State University Campus, the original park was located between Fourth and Seventh Streets, bordered by San Fernando Street to the north and San Carlos Street to the south. This 27 acre rectangular square was laid out in the original survey of the Pueblo by federal surveyor, Chester S. Lyman.

James Frazier Reed, a businessman and land speculator from Springfield, Illinois and an organizer of the famed Reed-Donner party, arrived in San Jose in the 1840s and immediately purchased large parcels of land east of the Pueblo in the vicinity of Washington Square. Reed had been instrumental in moving the Illinois State Capital from Vandalia to Springfield, and he now intended to promote San Jose as the site for the Capital of the new state of California. He was aware of the fact that the presence of the Capital would increase the importance of San Jose and the value of his adjacent land.

Reed put up a goodly portion of the money necessary to get the Legislature to come to San Jose and in return, the City Fathers deeded Washington Square to Reed. The Legislature spent one year in San Jose, but discouraged by cramped quarters and one of the rainiest winters on record, moved to Vallejo. In hopes that the the issue was not dead, Reed deeded the Square back to the City as a site for the Capitol Building. It was never to be, but the expectation of the return of the Capital was to persist well into the 20th Century.

Through the 1850s and 60s Washington Square lay undeveloped. The land was low and swampy, and the adobe soil did not encourage cultivation. It soon became an unofficial rubbish dump and one of the few areas in town where one could slaughter animals. Fourth Street became the right-of-way for the new railroad, and the collection of warehouses, drayage firms and lumber yards added to the area's scruffy appearance. The only sign of relief in the otherwise blighted neighborhood was General Naglee's estate, a lavish park which began at 11th Street.

The first improvement to the property came in the 1860s when the Washington Square School under the directorship of Fannie M. Price was constructed on the northeast corner at Seventh and San Fernando Streets. Still hoping for the return of the Capital, the City Fathers were somewhat assuaged by the possibility of acquiring the State Normal School for the Square.

The first State Normal School, a teacher's training institution, was established in San Francisco in 1857, but the rowdy "immoral" atmosphere of that city had convinced the State Board of Education that a more peaceful rural environment would be a more fitting place to educate young ladies. (The College of the Pacific and the College of Notre Dame would use the same rationale some years later when they decamped from San Jose for Stockton and Belmont respectively). Normal School Principal William Lucky, who favored San Jose over the other cities in the running, told the assembled citizens of San Jose that since Stockton had received the State Asylum for the Insane, San Jose should get the Normal School, and he went on to add that San Jose would became "synonymous with education as Stockton is synonymous with insanity." The San Jose *Mercury* assured their readers that: *Unlike a college or state university that attracts many fast and mischievous young men, not a desirable acquisition to any community, the*

*Normal School comprises only the most desirable of young people.*

The City of San Jose gratefully deeded Washington Square to the State for use as a Normal School in August 1870 but with the stipulation that should the school be moved, the land would revert to the City. The first Normal School building, an impressive three story structure, was soon built in the center of the Square facing west up San Antonio Street toward the Plaza. The grounds, however, remained, in the words of an early chronicler: *an unimproved and dreary waste. Students who climbed to the tower in those days will remember looking down on the network of irregular paths marked out to serve the inclination and convenience of daily foot travelers; and they will remember too, the few straggling trees and bushes.*

It was not until thirteen years later after fire had destroyed the first Normal School building that appropriations were made by the Legislature not only to rebuild, but also to properly drain, grade and ornament the grounds. Under the supervision of R. Ulrich, the landscape gardener who later became noted as the designer of the Del Monte Hotel grounds, Washington Square was transformed from an eyesore to a city attraction. As the environment of the Normal School changed, so did the surrounding neighborhoods which provided room and board and other services for the ladies and occasional gentlemen who would become the State's teachers.

The City too found the Square an agreeable place and in 1897 successfully petitioned to have San Jose High School located on the northern edge between Fifth and Seventh Streets. They came back in 1901 to request that the Andrew Carnegie Public Library be built on the corner of Fourth and San Fernando Streets. So even though the Square was State property, it still functioned very much as a city park up until the 1950s when the expanding State College pushed off the High School and later the Carnegie Library Building.

During the period of postwar expansion, the State architects encircled the Square with nondescript college buildings which closed the campus off from the City. The inner quad, however, with Tower Hall, fountain, tree-lined walks and superior landscaping, still remains and welcomes visitors who stray in from the tumult of Downtown San Jose. As the City becomes more densely populated with highrises and people, the campus, or Washington Square, may become once again a place for restful walks and contemplation. San Jose State University, in an attempt to recognize its beginnings has recently adopted "One Washington Square" as its address. It adds, you must admit, a touch of class.

*Second Normal School building, prior to the landscaping of Washington Square. Note the railroad tracks in foreground. San Jose State University Library Special Collections.*

# The San Jose Carnegie Library

*Andrew Carnegie 1837-1919. From* The Life of Andrew Carnegie *by Burton J. Hendrick.*

NOW THAT WE ARE approaching the centenary of the first Carnegie library buildings it seems an appropriate time to remember Andrew Carnegie and his contribution to the free public library movement in the United States.

Carnegie amassed a huge fortune (some said at the expense of his workers) by building the cartel which later became U.S. Steel. A Scottish immigrant who started out as a laborer, he was the embodiment of the Horatio Alger rags to riches hero. Through the Carnegie Foundation he distributed his wealth to a number of varied institutions worldwide. However, he is given the most recognition for the over $41 million he contributed for the construction of 1,649 library buildings, 1,412 of which were in the United States.

His up-by-the-bootstraps philosophy of self-reliance was reflected in his support of libraries: *I think it fruitful in the extreme, because it helps only those that help themselves, because it does not sap the foundation of manly independence, because it does not pauperize, because it stretches a hand to the aspiring and places a ladder upon which they can only ascend by doing the climbing themselves. This is not a charity, this is not philanthropy, it is the people themselves helping themselves by taxing themselves.*

The communities receiving library grants had to guarantee that they would assess themselves enough to stock, maintain and service each library. The amount awarded was based upon the population of the community. Grants in California ran from $2,500 (Concord) to over $700,000 for the San Francisco library system.

The first Carnegie library grant given in California was to the city of San Diego in 1899 for $60,000. In all, 142 buildings in 121 communities were funded in California until 1917 when the program ceased. By then practically every town and hamlet had its monument to culture and western civilization. In most cases local architects were selected, the exception being the plans for some of the smaller cities which were picked up by the firm of William Weeks.

Although the Carnegie people did not control architectural planning, there was a similarity in the layout of many of these structures. No matter what the scale, and some were quite small, they presented a facade of solidity. The arrangement and use of space inside was not always, however, the most efficient.

San Jose was not long in submitting its application for funds. In February 1901, O.H. Hale, local proprietor of the Hale's department store chain, wrote Mr. Carnegie: *The city of San Jose, California, contains a population of 25 to 30 thousand, and is essentially a city of homes, schools and churches. The Free Library is at present located on the second floor of the City Hall building directly over the Police Court and jail. Our people are exceedingly anxious to secure a new library and will furnish a free site in a small park in close proximity to the new Post Office Building. (Presumably Plaza Park.) The Mayor and Common Council are willing to pass an ordinance fixing the tax levy at a rate that will produce a revenue of 5 to 6 thousand dollars*

*Postcard courtesy of Jack Douglas.*

*per annum for permanent maintenance. Will you kindly advise if you are favorably inclined to donate to our city the sum of $50,000 for this purpose.*

The funds were granted and William Binder was selected to draw up the plans. (Binder and his partner E.N. Curtis, under the employ of developer T.S. Montgomery, would shortly change the face of downtown San Jose with their designs for the Twohy Building, the Civic Auditorium and many theatres, hotels and churches.)

The Plaza Park site was scrapped when the mayor convinced the state to give back a corner of Washington Square (part of the Normal School property) at Fourth and San Fernando Streets.

The laying of the cornerstone took place on Sunday, February 17, 1902 under the auspices of the local Elks Lodge. Not content with a simple ceremony, the Elks created a patriotic celebration that would rival the 4th of July pageants. A grand parade was formed at Second and Santa Clara Streets consisting of all 200 local Elks, each carrying an American flag. Also included was the Fifth Regimental Band, a platoon of police, members of the Common Council, library trustees and other city and county officials. The ceremony was almost entirely an Elks affair including speeches and prayers by the Exalted Ruler Joseph R. Patton and Chaplain Southgate. The orator of the day was attorney and past exalted ruler Jackson Hatch. (Hatch would single-handedly acquire a Carnegie grant for the city of East San Jose in 1907.)

At the conclusion of Hatch's lengthy address, Exalted Ruler Patton installed the cornerstone with its sealed box of items meant for the eyes of generations yet unborn. Included were recent copies of the local papers and numerous Elk's Club documents. To top off their contribution the cornerstone was engraved "Placed by the San Jose Lodge, No. 522 B.P.O.E. at the request of the Mayor and Common Council."

Everyone went home that day believing that they had witnessed a memorable event. And indeed they had, for the next day a storm of protest arose. The Pastor's Union, made up of most of the city's clergy, was infuriated over the manner in which the Elks had taken over the program. They objected to the holding of such an event on the Sabbath, they labeled as bad taste the Elks insertion of their insignia on the inscription, and they were appalled that no date or reference to Carnegie was included. It was, they said, "an insult to the sanity of the building."

To complicate the matter even more, the contractor, F.A. Curtis, removed the granite block, claiming that it was not included in his contract which had specified a plain sandstone block. While locked away in the contractor's tool shed the offending stone was mysteriously defaced. The Common Council finally left the decision of the inscription up to the architect. Binder, himself an Elk who was probably sorry he had ever invited them to the party, finally settled for the simple inscription "AD 1902." Curtis rewrote his contract, added $30 to the bill and installed the second cornerstone with only the workmen present.

The handsome, copper domed, neoclassical library was opened on June 1, 1903. The location in the park near the college and San Jose High was appealing, but the activity on the S.P. tracks which ran down Fourth Street must have been disconcerting to the readers.

The 1906 earthquake caused damage to a number of Carnegie libraries and the foundation granted funds to some cities for repairs, but San Jose was rejected. Rejection came again in 1921 when the librarian requested funds to add more rooms. As Mr. Woods, the librarian, put it: *The building erected by Mr. Carnegie's gift in 1902 has become entirely inadequate to serve a population which has grown from 21,000 in 1900 to 40,000 in 1920.*

The rapid growth of many California cities made most of the Carnegie buildings obsolete. By the 1930s many had been converted to other municipal uses. San Jose's was abandoned in 1937 when the library was moved to the vacated post office building at San Fernando and Market Streets (now the San Jose Art Museum). The solid little building was reputedly sold to the college for $55,000 and was converted into the student union or "Coop" as it was affectionately called by the thousands of students who passed through its doors for the next 23 years. It was razed in 1960 to make way, appropriately enough if not aesthetically enough, for an addition to the college library.

According to a study by Watsonville historian Betty Lewis, 33 California Carnegie buildings still function as libraries; 55 have been demolished and the rest have been converted to other uses. Many, such as the one in Gilroy, have been turned into museums.

It is difficult to measure the impact of Carnegie's gifts on the overall improvement of our citizens' cultural lives, but they allowed communities to take their libraries out of the drafty backrooms of city halls and rented quarters and make them into visible symbols of pride. For this we are in his debt.

In recognition of their importance, the State Office of Historic Preservation is processing papers to place existing Carnegie buildings on the National Register of Historic Places.

*The Margaret Pratt Home. Photo published in* Sunshine, Fruit and Flowers, *1896.*

# The Pratt Home

BY THE 1880S THE PIONEER SETTLEMENT OF SAN Jose had become a mature town of about 14,000 residents. With this growth came a need for institutions for the aid and comfort of orphans, indigents and old people.

Facilities such as the county hospital, the alms house (now Elmwood Jail) and Agnews State Hospital for the insane were established during this time.

In 1880 the Sheltering Arms Society was established to look to the needs of orphans and elderly women. A leader in these efforts was Mrs. Margaret Pratt, the widow of W.W. Pratt, a wealthy businessman and landowner in Almaden Township who had come to California during the gold rush. Mrs. Pratt contributed $9,000 toward the construction of a large three-story Queen Ann Victorian at 1159 South First (between Humbolt and Goodyear Streets). It was named the Pratt Home in recognition of her generous donation.

The home soon became a familiar local landmark. When the first Home of Benevolence was built at the corner of Eleventh and Margaret Streets, the orphans were transferred there, leaving the Pratt Home exclusively for elderly ladies. In the early days a flat fee of $1,000 entitled a resident to room and board and good personal care for life. Unfortunately, inflation and unexpected longevity of the tenants almost bankrupted the society. Raising fees to $2,000 only temporarily solved the upkeep problem.

In spite of its financial problems, the Pratt Home was a source of pride to San Joseans. A large photo of it appears in *Sunshine, Fruit and Flowers,* the 1896 pictorial souvenir book. The home was usually mentioned in the early city and county histories and guidebooks, and it was featured on an early penny postcard.

By the end of World War II the home had become woefully obsolete. New health and safety standards prohibited housing the elderly in creaky second floor frame buildings. It appeared that the structure would have to be abandoned. The board of directors found a better solution, however, by negotiating with the San Jose State College Corporation to turn the old home into a women's dormitory. An August 1945 issue of the *Mercury* describes the changeover: *The splendor of yesteryear is still prevalent in the faded tapestry and yellow wallpaper of the*

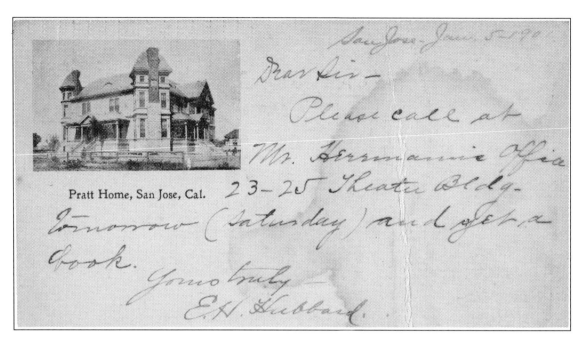

*Postcard dated Jan. 5, 1901 featuring the Pratt Home. Courtesy of Jack Douglas.*

*massive 60 room Pratt Home, which has housed the aged since 1889. And now, after more than 55 years of soft voices and the slow patter of slippered feet along numerous hallways, the home will resound with young laughter.*

Under the supervision of longtime chemistry professor, P. Victor Peterson, the college corporation spent almost $15,000 renovating and furnishing the home for student use. The long slides, which had served as fire escapes for over 50 years, were removed and iron stairs put in their places. The kitchen, which was designed to serve light food, had to be geared up to produce large quantities for 80 hungry coeds who ate three times a day, seven days a week. The women paid $45 per month or $135 per quarter for room and board.

Not all the rocking chairs were discarded, however, for five elderly tenants, aged 89 - 93, whose lifetime contracts hadn't run out, remained in the hall. Accepted as part of the community, they and their matron were reminders of the home's previous use.

Now called Pratt Hall, the new dorm rivaled the Catholic Women's Center (CWC) at Fifth and San Fernando in size and accommodation. It was SJS's first college operated dorm, offering an alternative to CWC, the sororities and privately run residence halls. The distance from campus, easily traversed by

city bus, gave an air of exclusivity. The distance also did not deter the beaus who gravitated there. One such suitor was former SJS Social Science Dean Dr. Charles Burdick whose wife to be, Katherine, was a Pratt girl. Dean Burdick remembers long lines of couples parting at the front entrance at curfew under the watchful eye of Mrs. Belle Moore, the Pratt housemother.

The hall published its own twice monthly newspaper called the *Prattler*. In its pages were pieces about the hall's parties and frequent engagement announcements. One of the big items in 1950 was a "five day quarantine which temporarily eliminated everyone's social life."

For reasons unclear to this writer, Pratt Hall was phased out in 1952. The Sheltering Arms Society, which still owned the building, sold it to Mr. Sylvan Le Deit Sr., a glass company owner who planned to raze it and develop the land. The hall was systematically dismantled (no bulldozers), but just as the work was almost finished, a fire, which started in rubbish, spread to the lumber piles, and most of the salvaged material was destroyed. So on June 3, 1952, a fire, which for generations had eluded this rambling wood-framed tinderbox, brought a spectacular close to another part of our history.

# St. James Square Historical District

THE ORIGIN OF ST. JAMES SQUARE DATES BACK TO the beginning of San Jose's American period (1848) when the city fathers commissioned the Yale educated surveyor Charles S. Lyman to lay out a plan for the future city of San Jose. Lyman reserved a large open area for public open space by combining twin rectangular blocks within the standard grid plan for the city. This area was called St. James Square. Twenty years later Frederick Law Olmsted, America's greatest pioneer landscape architect, laid out the diagonal and peripheral walkways. Plantings were begun. With this addition, St. James Square became officially known as St. James Park.

Over the years, beginning with the construction of the Trinity Episcopal Church in 1863, St. James Park has been the favored site of many of the city's distinguished churches and public buildings. Serenely set apart from the downtown commercial district, the park has been spared the periodic renovations and upheavals of the city's main street, and it remains one of the few areas in San Jose which reflects an earlier era. This was duly recognized in 1977 by the United States Department of the Interior, when the park and its surroundings were placed on the National Register of Historic Places.

Nine remaining buildings which surround St. James Park are designated National Register and San Jose Landmarks. They are:

## Trinity Episcopal Church. 1863

Trinity Episcopal Church is the oldest permanent Protestant church in San Jose. Constructed by John W. Hammond, it is one of the finest examples of carpenter Gothic religious architecture in the western United States. The interior of the church is very ornately carved redwood, with ornamented beams and trusses, and an exceptional

*Postcard courtesy of Jack Douglas.*

multi-Gothic arched chancel. Other features include beautiful stained glass windows crafted by the New York firm of Doremus, and the tower chimes which date from the 1860s.

## Santa Clara County Courthouse. 1866

Hoping to lure the state government back to San Jose, the city fathers proposed a courthouse so grandiose that it would have been possible to use it as a capitol building should such a move occur. Designed by Levi Goodrich, a pioneer architect who went on to build many important local structures, the courthouse was one of the most ornate and opulent civic buildings of its day. Designed along classical lines, the original building was two-storied with a central dome. A fire in 1933 led to the dome's removal and the addition of a third story. Renovated and restored in 1973, it continues to be one of the most impressive court buildings in the state.

Courthouse commenced in 1866 and finished in 1868. County jail was commenced in 1870 and finished in 1871. Picture taken between 1868 and 1870. Bare field at center right is St. James Park. Photo taken by J.H. Heering. San Jose Historical Museum Collections.

## First Unitarian Church. 1891

The First Unitarian Church was designed by local architect G.W. Page who had among his commissions many of the city's finer homes, including the Hayes mansion in Edenvale. The church, built in the Romanesque Revival style, was said to resemble a "Transylvanian Unitarian church." The unusual design includes such features as four domes, a large triple arched stained glass window on the facade and two towers flanking the main entrance. The central chapel is circular. The Unitarian congregation in San Jose has never been large, but the size and opulence of their church indicates that the members have been some of the city's most prominent and well-to-do citizens.

## Sainte Claire Club. 1893

The Sainte Claire Club was organized by Senator James D. Phelan as a meeting place for local businessmen. Phelan, a former mayor of San Francisco who spent the summers at his Villa

Montalvo in Saratoga, was also the owner of the Victory Theatre on North First Street. He chose San Francisco's leading pre-earthquake architect, A. Page Brown, to design the Sainte Claire Club. Best known as the architect of the San Francisco Ferry Building, Brown was a leading exponent of the Mission Revival architectural style. Many features of this style are evident in his design for the club, including the tile roof and arched entryways.

## Eagles Hall. 1900

Following the example of the Sainte Claire Club, the Masons chose to build their first temple facing St. James Park. This structure, which later became the home of the Eagles order, was one of the finest examples of Greek revival architecture in San Jose. The massive doric columns and the facade of the original building have been incorporated into the new office building which was constructed on the site of the hall.

## First Church of Christ Scientist. 1904

The First Church of Christ Scientist is one of the few examples in the South Bay of the work of

*Scottish Rite Temple now San Jose Athletic Club.*

architect Willis Polk. One of California's most famous architects, he designed the church along classical lines with modifications similar to those of Palladio. The ground floor plan of the church is in the shape of a Greek cross.

## Scottish Rite Temple. 1924

The local Masonic order, at first located in what we now refer to as Eagles Hall, commissioned Carl Werner to design a new temple at the corner of Third and St. James. The result was a massive three-story neo-classical structure with elements of Beaux Arts styling and Egyptian ornamentation. The massive facade with six ionic columns is consistent with several other buildings around the park, particularly the Courthouse which faces it on the west. Now the home of the San Jose Athletic Club, the exterior of the temple has been restored, and its maintenance has been assured.

## Letcher Garage. 1907

This garage, remodeled as the Oasis Night Club, was part of one of the first automobile showroom garages in San Jose. It was owned and operated by Clarence Letcher who was one of the city's earliest auto enthusiasts. It was acclaimed as the first auto garage on the west coast, and was to become the nucleus of San Jose's first automobile row. For a short while Letcher manufactured his own cars, but he gave that up to become the local dealer for Cadillac, Packard and Pierce Arrow. His "milepost" signs were familiar throughout the state for a quarter of a century.

The building has unique architectural features such as an expansive wood truss roof design and large steel shutters on the rear window openings.

## San Jose Post Office. 1933

The former main post office was a WPA project. It was built to replace the 1892 post office on Market Street. This newer structure, designed by Ralph Wykoff, incorporates many elements of Spanish Colonial Revival style, including terra cotta facing, churrigueresque ornamentation around the windows and doors, and red tile roof covering. The ornate

*Postcard courtesy of Jack Douglas.*

interiors add to a feeling of quality which is not evident in more recent government buildings. The post office is on the site of the former St. James Hotel, one of the city's leading hostelries dating from the 1890s.

# The Sainte Claire Club

THE 100TH ANNIVERSARY OF THE SAINTE CLAIRE CLUB, once the unofficial seat of power in the county, was celebrated in November 1988 with little public notice. This should be no surprise, for the exclusive men's organization, whose membership roster has included a veritable who's who of influential local business and professional men, has long cherished its privacy.

An early history describes the founding of the club: *At a gathering of the boys at the office of Wright and Field it was suggested by Mr. E.C. Reed that a Gentlemen's Club be organized in San Jose and for the purpose of getting things in shape Arthur Field moved that Mr. W.K. Beans act as President, Mr. A.G. Field was chosen as secretary, and upon the motion of Mr. A.W. Ingalsbe Mr. Beans appointed all the gentlemen present to see their friends and request them to meet at Wright and Field's office on Tuesday eve. Oct. 16th, 1888 and talk matters over. The following persons were present and promised to see their friends. Hon. Sam N. Rucker, A.W. Ingalsbe, E.C. Reed, A.K. Whitton and N.H. Castle.*

A few weeks later the "boys" had rounded up 72 friends and relations who became charter members. Being an organization of young men, there were few California pioneers represented, rather one might say that these were the "sons of the pioneers." One exception was banker T. Ellard Beans, who had arrived by wagon train in 1850. There were numerous family names which are familiar today — Tully, Clayton, Shortridge, Polhemus, Hobson, Murphy and Morgan Hill.

The Rucker clan was well represented by brothers James, Samuel and Joseph, all of whom were partners in their father's furniture business in the Rucker Building on North First. The club met in rented rooms in that building from 1889-1894. Sam Rucker, who served in the state assembly and was elected mayor of San Jose at the tender age of 25, was the club's second president.

The club's president during its first five years was Dr. Robert E. Pierce, prominent surgeon, who resided at the Vendome Hotel. Generally speaking, these men, if not established, were on the way up. It wasn't long before other important names appeared on the roster: Hart, Hale, Lion, Hanchett, Masson, and Oneal.

It was necessary to choose a name that spoke for location and also had distinction. They considered calling it the Santa Clara Club but thought better of naming their all male group after a female saint. They settled for St. Claire but before long lapsed into the feminine Sainte Claire. The name caught on and

was later appropriated by a number of businesses — Sainte Claire Hotel, Building, Cadillac agency, etc.

There was no shortage of social, fraternal or veterans organizations in San Jose of the 1880s, but the Sainte Claire members wanted to form an elite men's club comparable to the best in San Francisco such as the Pacific Union Club and the Bohemian Club. Unlike the latter, the Sainte Claire Club had no pretensions to literary or scholarly pursuits. Its primary activity was fellowship. There was probably more business transacted over the Sainte Claire card tables than any other place in town.

The club's permanence was assured when James D. Phelan became a member in 1893. A native of San Francisco and its reform mayor from 1897-1901,

*The Sainte Claire Club House, about 1896, two years after it opened. Courtesy Sainte Claire Club.*

Phelan also owned several major buildings on San Jose's First Street, including the Phelan Building (at Post St.), the Rucker Building and the Victory Theatre Building on North First. Phelan offered to construct a building to suit the club's needs which the members could then lease on generous terms. Recognizing the opportunity, the members quickly closed the deal.

The result was the beautiful building which stands at the corner of St. James and Second Street. The designer was A. Page Brown, a leading San Francisco architect and friend of Phelan. The club building and the San Francisco Ferry Building are about all that was left of Brown's work following the 1906 earthquake and fire.

One of the earliest examples of California Mission style, the Sainte Claire Club is one of the best preserved of the nine outstanding buildings which face St. James Park and make up our National Register Saint James Historic District. The symmetry of the building is carried through to the interior. Large rooms flank the central entry and staircase. The room on the right is the dining room where, in the beginning, the members were served three meals a day. To the left of the entry is the large social hall. Some very nice California landscapes adorn the walls. Above the dining room one will find the club bar and lounge which was tastefully remodeled in walnut paneling in 1970. A lounge and a library, with all the overstuffed accoutrements one associates with private clubs, are located on the second floor above the social hall. The third floor was devoted to sleeping rooms for members, a service which ceased in 1966.

During its 95 years of existence the clubhouse has suffered two catastrophes. The first was the '06 quake which threw slumbering residents out of their beds, collapsing some of the walls around them. Undeterred, the staff served breakfast outside at the back of the damaged building. Noted architect William Weeks was commissioned to restore the clubhouse (he also rehabilitated the Hotel Vendome).

A fire caused heavy damage to the club on

*The Sainte Claire Club Dining Room as it looks today. Courtesy Sainte Claire Club.*

February 24, 1949. George Fichtner, the only tenant in the building at the time, barely got out of the building alive. A slow burning fire in the kitchen chimney spread and engulfed most of the east wing. Apparently the evening card players had smelled the smoke but decided it was the result of their cigars.

Only on rare occasions have the members opened their doors to outsiders. During both world wars, military officers from local garrisons were welcomed as honored guests, and some were even billeted on the third floor for short periods. President McKinley was invited to accept the club's "privileges and courtesies" on his three day visit to San Jose in 1901, but there is no evidence that he got any closer than the rostrum across the street in St. James Park where he addressed the cheering crowds. Would-be president William Jennings Bryan was a guest, as were California governors Hiram Johnson and James Budd.

The period between the world wars were vexing for the club members. Wartime restrictions on alcohol were shortly carried over to all-out prohibition. Officially the club bar was closed, but the members were given lockers in the basement in which to stash their private bottles. A potent bathtub gin was also manufactured on the premises. Anti-gambling laws brought an end to the lucrative club slot machines. So popular were these devices that, before the ban, they were transported to club barbeques.

It seemed for a period in 1927 that the members would lose their clubhouse. Aging landlord Phelan had offered to deed the building to the county for use as an historical museum with the stipulation that if the building ceased to be used for a museum it would revert to the Phelan estate. The county supervisors refused the offer on these conditions and proved, once again, that history was not high on their agenda. After Phelan's death the Sainte Claire Club was given the opportunity to buy the building for $11,000. There must have been a great sigh of relief when, after 55 years, the tenants finally became the owners.

The postwar period brought great changes to San Jose and the valley. The agricultural based economy was replaced by large corporations with headquarters elsewhere. In the early days most of the members worked and or lived within a few blocks of the club, but during the 50s businesses and businessmen began to leave downtown for the suburbs where new family, social and cultural activities competed for their time. In spite of this, the club survived. As it moves into its second century there will no doubt be other challenges, not the least of which could be the issue of membership for women.

At the urging of the late Duncan Oneal, the club commissioned the noted author James D. Houston to write the *Centennial History of the Sainte Claire Club, 1888 - 1988*. The limited edition for members and a few libraries was recently published. This volume supplied much of the information for this article.

# The Letcher Garage: Scene of Triumph and Tragedy

IN THE ROSTER OF historic buildings surrounding St. James Park (the County Courthouse, the Scottish Rite Temple-San Jose Athletic Club, Trinity Church, etc.), the uninitiated are amazed to see the old Four Wheel Brake Garage (now the Oasis night club) at the corner of First and St. James among the elect. Few realize the important role this ordinary looking garage played in the automotive history of Santa Clara County. It was also the scene of what was probably the most sensational event in San Jose's history, prior to the infamous lynchings in 1933.

The Four Wheel Brake Garage and the garage building next door (which has recently been converted into several Vietnamese shops) were built between the years of 1906 and 1908 by Clarence Letcher. In 1900, Letcher, who was one of California's first auto enthusiasts, owned and operated, at Market and San Carlos, what was acclaimed to be the first automobile garage on the West coast. Prior to Henry Ford's development of the cheap assemblyline auto production, many autos were built locally by enterprising tinkerers. Clarence Letcher, Frank and Arthur Holmes, George Osen and William Hunt all made custom built autos in the late 1890s; the latter team built their flivvers at the rear of their bicycle shop at 69 South Second Street.

Clarence Letcher was the first to see that the real opportunities were in the maintenance and repair of the ever increasing number of cars in the Valley. By 1906, Letcher had outgrown the Market and San Carlos facility and had moved into the new garage at North First and St. James. Letcher, no longer a car builder, now became a dealer of Detroit built luxury cars: Cadillac, Packard and Pierce Arrow.

Among his many other pioneering achievements can be added: the first gasoline station, the first rental cars in the Valley, and the first major statewide advertising campaigns for these various services.

Long before Burma Shave and Anderson Split Pea roadside advertising, California motorists throughout the state were greeted everywhere by colorful milepost signs announcing the number of miles to San Jose's Letcher Garage. Not since the heyday of General Henry Naglee's famous brandy, had the West's attention been so focused, through advertising, on the city of San Jose.

Hardly had he moved into his new facility, when Letcher began planning an even more elaborate garage and showroom next door. The new building, designed by Wolf and McKenzie, was in the popular Mission style, with room for offices above the front entrance. Sketches of the proposed building were shown in a Fall 1907 issue of the *Mercury Herald*. Sometime between the building's construction and the 1914 photo (next page) the structure took on a modified English Tudor appearance. When Letcher moved into the new building, Osen and Hunter purchased the corner location from Letcher for their Dodge dealership.

During his early success, Letcher divorced his first wife, by whom he had had his only child, George Truman Letcher, and married Helen Permian. After living for a time in the affluent Naglee Park neighborhood, the Letchers purchased a ranch in the Santa Cruz Mountains. They also kept a suite at the Vendome Hotel, three blocks from the garage, for use while in town. With business doing so well, Clarence was able to devote a good deal of his time to local politics, the Elks and Exchange Clubs, and various outdoor activities. His closest friend and attorney was Louis Oneal, a local rancher and powerful political figure. Letcher was also a neighbor and friend of San Francisco Mayor and later Governor "Sunny" Jim Rolph.

By the mid-twenties, the Letchers' marriage had

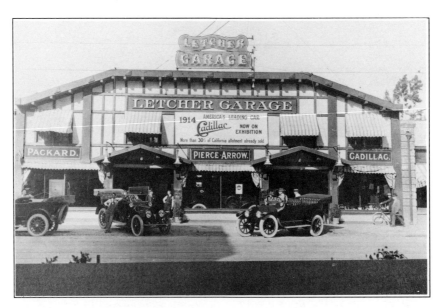

*Letcher's Garage as it appeared in 1914. San Jose Historical Museum Collections.*

fallen on hard times: Clarence was maintaining a separate domicile in the old Saint James Hotel, and was keeping company with Mrs. Ann Bennett, a blond divorcee who worked in a local beauty salon. Helen Letcher had confronted her husband about this affair on several occasions, and each time came to an amicable agreement with him. On the afternoon of July 2, 1926, after spending the day with her favorite niece, who coincidentally lived in the same Reed Street apartment building as Mrs. Bennett, Helen drove to the garage for what was to be her final attempt to, as the newspapers described it, "regain her husband's love."

Letcher and his wife spoke briefly at the entrance of the garage while men worked on a scaffold just above their heads. Garage employees and people on the street were surprised when a series of shots rang out, and Clarence Letcher was seen alternately trying to dodge the fusillade of bullets and wrest the 38 revolver from his wife's hand. Two non-fatal shots struck him in the head causing him to stagger to the rear of the garage where he fell into the arms of an employee. Mrs. Letcher, undeterred, fired again at her husband and the bullet struck him just below the heart. In a final act of anguish, she brushed away her hat and shot herself in the temple.

Clarence Letcher was driven, still conscious, to the San Jose Hospital where he lingered until the fol-

lowing day. A young reporter, Theron Fox, was on the scene in time to help put the lifeless body of Helen Letcher into an ambulance. The front page of Saturday's *Mercury Herald* prominently displayed a photo montage of Clarence, Helen and the "other woman" Mrs. Ann Bennett, with the title: "Double Tragedy Closes Marital Differences."

Helen's outraged relatives tried, to no avail, to bring criminal proceedings against Mrs. Bennett who had gone into hiding. It was with great effort that Letcher's attorney, Louis Oneal, convinced the distraught relatives that Clarence and Helen should be laid to rest side by side in a double burial at Oak Hill.

Fate stepped in, however, to separate them forever. Shortly after the burial service, conducted by the Elks Lodge and attended by such luminaries as Oneal and Mayor Rolph, Mr. Letcher's will was discovered. In the will, Letcher had requested that his remains be cremated and the ashes spread over Mt. Hamilton. The bodies were disinterred to carry out Clarence's wishes, and Helen was buried beside her mother in an Oakland cemetery.

Prominently displayed on the sign above the entrance to the Letcher Garage was an illustration of the ubiquitous milepost marker with a zero painted on it, along with the words: "The End of the Road." And so it was for Clarence Letcher.

# Camp Almaden: Our C.C.C. Outpost

Back in 1933 President Franklin D. Roosevelt launched his campaign to bring the nation out of the Great Depression. Among the alphabet soup of New Deal programs: NRA, WPA, TVA, FWP, etc, the CCC or Civilian Conservation Corps is, possibly, the most fondly remembered.

In its relatively short life (1933-1942) over 3,000,000 young men were given an opportunity to work, improve their general education, learn discipline, acquire practical job skills and travel to other parts of the country. As President Roosevelt put it in a speech delivered on July 17, 1933: *Through you the nation will graduate a fine group of strong men, clean living, trained to self discipline and, above all, willing and proud to work for the joy of working.* Putting to work millions of unemployed, unskilled and sometimes undernourished youth was the most obvious advantage of the CCC, but built into it was a welfare program to help the families of the enrollees. Each enrollee earned $30 a month, $25 of which was automatically sent to his parents.

The CCC camps were managed by the U.S. Army. Enrollees were formed into companies of approximately 200 men and were put under the supervision of military officers, usually a Captain assisted by a Lieutenant. Work was done under the supervision of the U.S. Forest Service and other conservation agencies. Our local camps were placed under the California Division of Forestry.

The Santa Clara County camp (project 234) was established at Inspiration Point on Mt. Madonna in June of 1933. Although it offered beautiful views, the water supply was not adequate to service a camp of over 250 people. The Division of Forestry decided to move the camp to Mine Hill above the village of New Almaden. The site was the abandoned village known as Englishtown. During the heyday of the quicksilver mines this settlement housed the Cornish miners who were brought in to dig out the mercury-rich cinnabar.

The first CCC company, 1917-V, was a hybrid group made up primarily of World War I veterans from Los Angeles. One exception was Omar Margason, a young San Jose man recently graduated

*Mine Hill Schoolhouse. Courtesy of Friedolin Kessler.*

from San Jose High. He was one of the first CCC enrollees from San Jose. The company was charged with determining which of the dilapidated buildings could be serviceable for camp use and which needed to be removed. Margason remembers that 41 houses were dismantled. The men lived in tents until a group of carpenters from San Jose put up the tar paper covered barracks and garages that would serve a succession of companies.

The company was also busy with improving the roads to the camp and clearing fire trails. They moved and reassembled the large "Mount Madonna CCC" camp gateway sign to the entrance of the Almaden camp thus adding to the confusion of nomenclature for the site. Since it was on the records in Washington as project 234 Camp Mt. Madonna, it continued to be identified as such even though the locals referred to it correctly as Camp Almaden. The name of the camp newspaper, *The Mt. Madonna Miner* added further to the confusion.

The veterans group left Camp Almaden in October 1934 and was followed by company 1235 from New Jersey and New York. They left in April 1935 for the camp at Priest River, Idaho. The camp was then occupied briefly by a group from company 1954 at the Pinnacles. In October 1935, company 3325, Pennsylvania recruits, arrived from Fort Monroe. They were to be the beneficiaries of a new program.

The December 7th issue of the *Mercury Herald* carried a feature story by G.H. McMurry: *Almaden College flourishes at old quicksilver camps: 200 CCC youths from Pennsylvania building trails and citizenship.* The occasion for the article was the official opening of "Almaden University" organized by Mr. George Forbes, camp educational advisor. A choice of

21 subjects were offered either by on-site staff or teachers brought in from San Jose and San Jose State College. There were also a number of correspondence courses available.

Company 3325 had hardly settled down before they were shipped out in January 1936. Their replacements were the men of company 739 from Missouri who would remain until October 1937. Camp routines and programs were established during their relatively long occupation. Under the command of Navy lieutenant R.G. Budwin the camp became a real community with its own school, library, athletic teams, clubs and a drama group that wrote and produced plays. Friedolin Kessler, San Jose artist and resident after his CCC discharge, was recruited out of art school to be the company artist. His main function was to document life in the camp and to preserve a record for officials in Washington. As camp artist he was responsible for doing the graphics for their award winning camp newspaper *The Mt. Madonna Miner* which was acclaimed by none other than Eleanor Roosevelt.

The company was kept very busy during the fall of '36 fighting grass and forest fires from Mt. Hamilton to Aptos and the Pacheco Pass. The worst, that dry season, was near the Gilroy Hot Springs where 100,000 acres burned for 10 days before it was controlled. Besides the fire duty, the men spent whole weeks working out of base or "spike" camps at Mt. Madonna, Smith Creek, Aptos and Hollister where they built fire lookout towers, cleared fire trails, installed telephone lines and constructed ranger stations. After the fire season was over they had time for trips to Santa Cruz for days of deep sea fishing and to San Francisco for the opening of the Golden Gate Bridge.

Almaden locals such as Connie Perham took the boys to their hearts and frequently attended the camp movies, plays and other social activities. San Jose groups — the Junior Chamber of Commerce for example — hosted social functions. One such, a dance at St. Joseph's School with music supplied by the WPA orchestra, was less than a success due to the awkwardness of the boys.

Several men from this company took employment in the San Jose area when they were discharged (two years was the maximum enlistment). They included, in addition to Friedolin Kessler, Robert Boston, Wilbur Duke, Ernest Pope and Donald Wood. One wonders if they, or any others, are still living in the area.

Company 450 from Alabama, Georgia and

*Artwork and photos in this article are from the collection of Friedolin Kessler.*

Florida replaced the Missourians and remained at Camp Almaden until November 1939 when they were transferred to Camp Rancho Solis near Gilroy in order to make way for the resumption of mercury production for the coming war effort. The spike camp at Inspiration Point on Mt. Madonna was turned over to the Boy Scouts.

The war and the need for workers of all kinds signaled the end of the CCC, but the boys who became men in its ranks have not forgotten what was for many a peak experience in their lives.

On October 10, 1992, the local chapter of the National Association of CCC Alumni dedicated a monument to the organization on Mine Hill, New Almaden. Designed by Friedolin Kessler, who supervised the construction of the work, this monument includes a plaque and the original camp flagpole. It is made of local stone and the bricks from the old Englishtown store. The CCC alumni in conjunction with the New Almaden Park Association had a pioneer day celebration after the unveiling of the monument.

*Mineral Spring Fountain, Alum Rock Park, San Jose, California.*
*Postcard courtesy of Jack Douglas.*

# Hot Springs Fever

FEVER FOR GOLD AND SILVER BROUGHT MEN FROM all over the world to primitive settlements in northern California. They toiled day and night through extreme weather conditions and grimiest circumstances. To them a warm bath must have been the ultimate luxury. Perhaps that is one of the reasons why the numerous hot spring sites began to flourish just as the dust was settling from the gold rush era. It is almost as if Californians traded gold fever for the high temperatures induced by our mineral springs.

Hot spring baths go back to earliest times. The appropriately named mineral springs resort of Bath in England was established by the Romans. Spas in Europe were all the rage until World War I. Many place names in California were borrowed from popular eastern hot spring resorts, including our own county's Saratoga and Congress Springs.

A book published in 1890 titled: *Mineral Springs and Health Resorts of California* by Winslow Anderson M.D. listed 198 mineral spring resorts in the state. Santa Clara County could boast seven such establishments — the major ones, which are described below, were Alum Rock Springs, Pacific Congress Springs and Gilroy Hot Springs. There were smaller operations in New Almaden, Madrone, Azule and Blodgett Springs.

## Alum Rock Mineral Springs

The Alum Rock Mineral Springs Hotel was well established prior to the city of San Jose's annexation of the "Reservation" (early name for Alum Rock Park) in 1872. Anderson's guide described it: *There springs are located in a romantic cañon with the unromantic name "Penitentiary Cañon," on the western slope of the Coast Range, about seven miles northeast of San Jose. ...The drive to San Jose is one of unusual grandeur...presenting an ever varying scene of ruggedness and natural beauty.*

Alum Rock had (has) over 20 separate springs including sulphur springs for bathing and soda springs for drinking. The 85° F sulphur springs were touted as ameliorating a variety of ills including anemia, chlorosis, chronic malaria, nervous prostration and debility.

The Alum Rock Springs Hotel burned to the ground in February 1890, but the city-supported bath house continued to minister to the numerous visitors who came up by train for the day. The outdoor grottos, many of which remain today, were built between 1890 and 1916. The mineral spring fountain is one of the oldest man-made landmarks in the park. With the construction of the Natatorium (covered swimming pool) in 1916, the public's interest in the hot springs was diverted to cool water activities and other features of the park.

## Pacific Congress Springs

The Pacific Congress Springs near Saratoga began as a private retreat in 1864 but was purchased in 1872 by Lewis P. Sage for $25,000 and opened to the public. It wasn't long before a rail line was bringing in swarms of visitors for extended stays. Congress Springs, with its elegant hotel and lush surroundings, was the closest thing we had to an eastern spa. The mineral content of the water, which was bottled and distributed throughout the state, was almost identical with that of Congress Springs, New York.

Anderson's guide described it as: *among the finest in the state, everything is first class, entertaining and pleasing, and thousands of people go there yearly for health and recreation.* It all came to an abrupt end on June 15, 1903 when the hotel burned to the ground.

## Gilroy Hot Springs

Gilroy Hot Springs has had the longest history of any resort in the area. Established in the 1870s by rancher George Roop, it functioned to some degree until 1980. In 1879 Roop built a three story hotel which included, in addition to the 32 furnished rooms, a large parlor, dining room and billiard room. There was also a 17 room annex to the hotel and 19 cottages. The grounds were landscaped with flowers and a bubbling fountain. A small village in itself, the Springs had its own post office and livery stable.

Visitors arrived in Gilroy on the twice daily train from San Francisco. They were picked up by a horse drawn stage. Later a Stanley Steamer was used.

Dr. Anderson had this to say: *Gilroy has one main spring which flows in great abundance. The temperature varies from 108° F to 115° F. This is light alkalo-sulphurous water, and is used with considerable benefit*

*in syphilis, rheumatism, scrofula and glandular swellings, chronic skin eruptions, etc.* Advertisements for the Springs emphasized that it was not a sanitarium and was not suitable for "consumptives."

Hunting, fishing, hiking and riding were popular pastimes for those less sedentary. A six mile bridal path to the Madrone Hot Springs was one of the resort's main attractions, as well as its "Trail of the Lonesome Pine" which was featured on a picture postcard from 1900.

Hot Springs Hotel, Gilroy, California. Postcard courtesy of Jack Douglas.

A major overhaul of the premises took place in 1913. A garage, gas station and better roads made the resort more amenable to the automobile age. An outdoor swimming pool, large deck and dressings rooms were added in 1917.

By the 1920s hot springs fever had definitely cooled. When the Southern Pacific discontinued its runs to Gilroy in 1932 the springs were destined to be used only by weekenders who came by car. W.J. McDonald, who had purchased the resort from Roop in 1924, sold it in 1938 to H.K. "Harry" Sakata of Watsonville who revived it as a spa for the area's Japanese-American population. A number of prominent Japanese-American businessmen from San Francisco built private cottages for their families during this period.

The resort was closed during World War II, and when it reopened in 1945 it operated only on a marginal basis. In 1980 the historic hotel, annex and several cottages went up in a giant blaze. The remaining structures have succumbed to earthquake, weather and vandalism.

Developers from Japan have purchased the site with the idea of building a large mineral springs resort. Should they succeed, we may see a revival of hot springs fever.

# Art and Connoisseurship in Early San Jose

A PROUD ANDREW JACKSON GRAYSON GAZES OUT OF the canvas at his viewers. He is clad in buckskins. His wife and child sit beside him on the ground, and in the background loom the Sierras.

This painting, titled: "The Promised Land," was the cornerstone of a 1992 exhibit: "Landmarks of Early California Painting" at the Crocker Museum in Sacramento. The sweep of this painting and the others

*William Smith Jewett's "The Promised Land," 1850. Photo is from* California History, *Spring 1992.*

---

*Alexander Edouart's "Blessing of Enrequita Mine, New Almaden, California, 1860." Photo from* California History, *Spring, 1992.*

in the show is breathtaking. Not only are they beautiful works in their own right, but they are also precious documents of our California landscape in its virgin state. They reflect the effect of our natural wonders, such as the Yosemite Valley, on the artists, and they show us how the artists chose to represent such subjects to skeptical easterners who would not have the privilege to visit the West until the completion of the transcontinental railroad in 1869.

The gold rush of '49 attracted many talented artists to northern California. Most came for gold but found their fortune practicing their art. The nouveau riche of the gold fields and San Francisco were eager customers for portraits and paintings depicting their exploits during those early years. By 1870 there were already feelings of nostalgia for the West that was and would never be again. A number of these patrons became connoisseurs of western art, filling their Nob Hill mansions with huge landscapes by premier western artists such as Thomas Hill, Frederick Butman, Virgil Williams, Charles Christian Nahl, William Hahn, Albert Bierstadt and William Keith, all of whom were represented in the Crocker Museum show. Fortunately, early western art collector, Edwin B. Crocker, kept his collection in Sacramento thus

avoiding the fate of so many important paintings that were destroyed in the earthquake and fire of '06.

Andrew Jackson Grayson was probably San Jose's first art connoisseur/patron. A man of many parts, he crossed the plains in 1846, just ahead of the Donner party. He served as an officer under Fremont, made a small fortune in commerce, then settled in San Jose to take up his real love, the painting of birdlife in the western slope. (see: "Andrew Jackson Grayson: Audubon of the West.") Grayson commissioned William Smith Jewett, a forty niner from New England, to do the classic painting of himself and his family.

A born naturalist, Grayson reveled in the primitive land that the average pioneer considered, at best, tedious. He wrote: *A still happier change awaited us when we at length passed, uninterrupted by the Indians, through the silent woods of the Sierra Nevada and beheld for the first time the promised land of our hopes - no words are adequate to express my feelings of delight, and most profound gratitude to my maker for thus leading us in His divine providence to so beautiful a land.*

Grayson took Jewett to the spot above Georgetown where this event occurred so that he

*John Ross Key's painting of grape pickers in General Naglee's vineyard, 1877. Photo from Clyde Arbuckle's* History of San Jose.

might accurately sketch the details of the impressive landscape. Grayson is said to have paid the princely sum of $2,000 for the painting.

There was another canvas in the Crocker show that is of local interest. It is Alexander Edouart's "Blessing of the Enrequita Mine, New Almaden, California, 1860." The scene documents the blessing of the mine by Father Goetz of San Jose and includes a panoply of characters, the mine owner, his family, the managers and the Mexican miners. The tree stumps and barren hills illustrate how the area was stripped to provide fuel for cooking the cinnebar. Edouart (1818-1892) was born in England and trained in Scotland and Italy before arriving in California in 1852.

Andrew Jackson Grayson may have been the first San Josean to value fine art, but it was not long before others with wealth and taste began taking an interest in collecting art for their palatial homes. General Henry M. Naglee, who was raised among the Philadelphia elite, collected a number of fine paintings on his many trips to the east and Europe. A civil war veteran, he was no doubt familiar with artist John Ross Key's many sketches of the war when he commissioned him to paint the grape pickers in his

vineyard in 1877. This pastoral scene on the banks of the Coyote Creek beautifully captures the time and place. According to Clyde Arbuckle, in his *History of San Jose*, Naglee offered his art collection to the City of San Jose, but the frugal city fathers, who couldn't imagine what to do with it, turned him down.

Mr. and Mrs. Myles P. O'Connor were formidable collectors of European art, making their mansion at Second and Reed an impressive gallery. When they gave up their home to the Sisters of Notre Dame for an orphanage, they too offered the collection to the City and, as in the Naglee case, were rebuffed. They eventually gave the collection to Trinity College in Washington D.C. and threw in $200,000 for a building to house it.

Mrs. Sarah Knox Goodrich, tireless worker for women's rights, wasted no time in acquiring the marble sculptures of Edmonia Lewis when they were exhibited at City Market Hall during Fair Week in 1873. Lewis, one of America's first celebrated black artists, received glowing notices in the *San Jose Weekly Mercury* and the *Patriot*. Three of the works exhibited, "Asleep," "Awake" and "Lincoln" are now owned by the San Jose Public Library.

Judge John Henley Moore (1825-1909), who was

active in local business as well as state and local politics, was another proud pioneer who collected western art. His giant portrait, artist unknown, hangs in the stairwell of the Pacific Hotel at the San Jose Historical Museum. His heirs donated paintings by William Keith (1838-1911) and Gideon Jacques Denny (1830-1886) along with other artworks to San Jose State College in 1951. Denny specialized in dark brooding seascapes and maritime subjects. Keith, a friend of James D. Phelan, exhibited works in the California gallery of the Chicago World's Fair in 1893.

Coming on the scene later, San Jose's triumvirate of western artists, Andrew P. Hill (1853-1922), Astley D.M. Cooper (1856-1924) and Charles H. Harmon (1859-1936), carried on the tradition of the pioneer landscape painters.

It is to the early painters, however, that we own a debt of gratitude. Through their works we share the awe and wonderment of the pioneers who first experienced the beauty of the unspoiled California landscape.

# A Tourist Guide History of San Jose and Environs

SINCE THE DAYS OF MARCO POLO, TRAVELERS HAVE relied upon guidebooks to tell them what to see in foreign climes. As a consequence, travel guides from the early Baedekers to the current Fromers are goldmines of information on what is or was currently fashionable in a particular place. For instance, who, in 1940, would ever have guessed that swarms of Japanese tourists would come to the Santa Clara Valley to take pictures of the single car garage where Hewlett and Packard invented the microchip. Times change and so do attitudes of what is important to visit in a given locale.

I've done a survey of available tourist guides of California going back to 1870 to see what features the writers thought worth noting in San Jose and our valley. Many of these sights no longer exist, but they live on in the early tourist guides and are piquant reminders of our colorful history.

In 1870, *Appleton's Handbook of American Travel, Western Tour*, describes San Jose as: *a busy town in the heart of the Santa Clara Valley, having 9,091 inhabitants. It is rapidly growing, and is a place of frequent resort for San Franciscans, who generally make their excursions here on Saturdays and Sundays. ... It contains one of the best appointed hotels on the coast, and its Court House, which cost $200,000 is considered the handsomest structure of its kind in the State. The view from the dome of this latter building is very fine. There are many productive vineyards and orchards in the town. In consequence of its healthful climate, which is a mean between the harsh winds of the coast and the hot valleys of the interior, San Jose and its neighborhood are much visited by those having pulmonary complaints.*

Appleton, who may never have actually visited San Jose, frequently quotes from an article in the *Springfield Republican* which describes the people in San Jose: *We see an American with his fine broad-*

*Vendome Hotel c. 1915. San Jose Historical Museum Collections.*

cloth and silk hat, his light wagon and well groomed trotter; there two or three rancheros with their slouched hats, loose and shabby garments, on rough-coated horses, stained with the mud of a former day; here a Mexican on a compactly limbed mustang with the high peak and broad stirrups of the Mexican saddle (which is the only one in use here) with his big broad-brimmed hat, his loose but jaunty jacket, with all the seams of his clothing trimmed with rows of small steel or silver buttons, and heavy spurs.

The commentator from the *Republican* goes on at some length upon the variety of races and nationalities in San Jose: *Chinese and negroes abound among the passersby on foot. There is a street in San Jose occupied entirely by the French. The houses are unpretending, but very cheerful and pretty, with small grounds a good deal decorated, abundance of flowers, and always a cluster of artichoke plants in the garden.* San Jose's pre-fire Chinatown is described thusly: *There is another quarter occupied entirely by Chinese; one story brick buildings, crowded and poor, but quaint with Chinese pottery, and brightened by what are called Chinese lil-*

lies, bulbs grown in dishes filled with pebbles and water. They are the narcissus of the spring borders in New England, and every Chinaman tries to have one blossom for his New Year's.

Appleton goes on to say: *An old adobe church in the town, built by the early Spanish missionaries, has been enclosed by brick to preserve it. There are some fine oil paintings to be seen at this place, among them being a superb copy of Murillo's "Repentant Peter" and one of Raphael's "Madonna del Seggiola." An excellent school kept by the Sisters of the Order of Notre-Dame is located here. It is worth visiting.*

The anonymous reporter from the *Republican* is quoted again as he rhapsodizes over the Santa Clara Valley: *I wish I could paint this beautiful valley as I saw it; its centre filled with the towns of San Jose and Santa Clara, its horizon bounded by mountains whose hollows were pink and brown in the morning sun and purple and blue in the sunset light. Some of them wooded, some bare, the foot hilly, with nooks suggesting lovely spots for country homes.*

The visitor is also advised to see the estate of

General Naglee with its beautiful gardens and trees imported from throughout the world. Naglee's brandy making operation is also described. In addition, many paragraphs are devoted to the New Almaden quicksilver mines.

The *Souvenir of San Jose and Vicinity*, a pictorial guide compiled by Crockwell and William in 1894, gives the reader a feeling for how quickly the valley was being settled even then: *So thickly is the country around settled that a bird's eye view detects with difficulty where the city ends and the suburbs or adjoining towns begin. Three lines of railroad, with fourteen passenger trains daily each way, connect San Jose with San Francisco — two broad gauge and one narrow gauge — besides a water route via the bay. Finely equipped electric railroads traverse the principal streets and connect the suburbs as far as Santa Clara, running here along the historic Alameda, an avenue as beautiful as it is venerable.*

By 1894 the observatory on Mount Hamilton had become a major attraction: *To the east, on the summit of the coast range, the eye discerns a white speck, the dome of the famous Lick Observatory. Here is harbored the greatest telescope, the most perfect astronomical instruments and apparatus ... a fine wagon road leads up to Mt. Hamilton, revealing beautiful vistas at every turn.*

Facilitated by the railroads, tourism was in full swing by 1890, and: *The Hotel Vendome, a palatial house in the heart of a fine residential section, is a favorite stopping place for tourists and coign of departure for the many points of interest around.*

*Rider's California*, a 1925 guide designed primarily for railroad tourists, provides a map of downtown and many details about the city. Rates for the various hotels are listed — room and bath at the Vendome was $3.50, at the Montgomery $2.50. For diners they suggest the Bohemia Cafe at 53 North First (Italian and French dinners), the Liberty Grille at 56 West Santa Clara St. (Sunday dinner $1.25), the American Grill at 258 South First (oysters and shellfish a specialty), and the Royal Cafeteria at 79 South First. Seven theatres are listed: the Victory on North First (best road attractions and vaudeville), the American (also vaudeville), and the Liberty, California, Lyric, Jose and Rex for motion pictures. Churches, banks, rail lines and motor stage lines are also listed.

Perhaps the most well-known tour guides of all were the WPA Guides. Compiled during the Great

Depression by the Federal Writer's Project arm of the Works Progress Administration, these thoroughly researched, well-written tourbooks describe the important features of most of our states. The *California Guide,* which has recently been reprinted in paperback by Pantheon Books, is a rich source of information and illustration of what our state was like in the 1930s.

The main points of interest for San Jose in this guidebook are: City Hall Park (one of the many names for the Plaza on Market Street) the Civic Auditorium, St. James Park (with a brief note about the 1933 lynching), and the County Court House. Another important local site at this time was the Edwin Markham Home (now at the Historical Museum). The Southern Pacific Station, through which many visitors arrived, had only recently been built (1936). *It is designed in a modified mission style, modernized by bronze doors and window frames. In the waiting room is a mural by J. MacQuarrie depict-*

*ing an early California scene, with skyscrapers and a railroad train in the background.*

The Rosicrucian Park, with its Egyptian Temple, Oriental Museum, Planetarium and Amenhotep Shrine, loom large as unique San Jose attractions, as does the Municipal Rose Garden for which: *Mrs. Fremont Older gave bushes from 18 of the 21 California mission gardens.* Alum Rock Park, the New Almaden Village and Quicksilver Mines and Lick Observatory are mentioned as points of interest. The Winchester Mystery House gets only a brief mention, being the: *externalization of a psychopathic mind.*

Old tourist guidebooks are a wonderful way to explore the past and to learn what kinds of attractions appealed to previous generations. They are also reminders of the many man made and natural wonders which still make this place the Valley of the Heart's Delight.

# Santa Clara County Goes To The World's Columbian Exhibition: Chicago, 1893

SANTA CLARA COUNTY PLAYED A PART IN THE world's fair celebration of the 400th anniversary of Columbus's voyage to America. Many local manufacturers, growers and artists contributed to the colorful California exhibit which highlighted our state's growing importance to the nation.

Set in a Chicago reborn from the disastrous fire of 1871, the fair was conceived by its planners to prove that this formerly backwoods region could create a rival to the antiquity of Europe in its culture and grandiosity. The plan, by the great landscape architect Frederick Law Olmsted, included a lake-

*California State Building (144x435 feet) at the World's Columbian Exposition, Chicago, 1893.*
*Photo courtesy of Jack Douglas.*

*Prune Horse from the Santa Clara Valley.*

side setting with canals and lagoons that would be compared to those of Venice. The massive exhibit halls, derived from classic Beaux-Arts designs, featured miles of domes, arches and columns, all in gleaming white. The scale and consistency of the architectural style has never been, or perhaps will never be, rivaled.

Two important themes set this fair apart from its predecessors: the emphasis on the arts, and the prominence of women in the organization and exhibits. Previous fairs had emphasized the latest scientific and engineering wonders and the inevitable march of progress during the 19th century. The Columbian Exhibition's White City was a work of art in itself. It glorified architecture as a reigning influence on our lives and gave a boost to the "City Beautiful" movement that changed the face of many American cities. There was an abundance of art galleries, horticultural halls and gardens. Women had their own building in which were displayed many of the so-called feminine arts.

The fair extolled the wealth and culture of the western states, and California outstripped every state but Illinois in the size and opulence of its building. San Francisco architect A. Page Brown rejected Greco-Roman models and created instead what some historians consider our first modern building based upon Spanish and Mission architectural styles. The tile roof, campanile and arched entrances would be copied on countless buildings for the next 30 years.

Two California planning boards, one of men and one of women, were formed to organize the state's participation. The president of the women's group was Mrs. E.O. Smith of San Jose who was a force in the local women's movement. A Unitarian, Democrat and Political Equality Club member, she was editor-in-chief of the weekly *Report* which espoused feminist causes.

Santa Clara County, the state's most fructuous region, had one of the largest exhibit spaces in the California Building. Fruits of all kinds, dried, fresh and in solution were on display for the millions of easterners to marvel at. On September 9th, sample packages of dried fruit were given out to every one of the 231,530 visitors who entered the exposition grounds. The county's wines were also prominently displayed.

James Duval Phelan was chosen the vice president of the California World's Fair Commission. This was to be the beginning of a life of public service which included three terms as mayor of San Francisco and one term in the U.S. Senate. A gifted public speaker, he gave the introductory address at the dedication of the California Building on June 19th and the welcoming speech at the equally important California Admission Day ceremonies on September 9th.

The manager of the Santa Clara County agricultural exhibit was Colonel Richard P. McGlincy who was president of the Campbell Fruit Growers Union and a leading fruit drier and packer. The assistant exhibit manager was Mrs. John McNaught, secretary of the San Jose Board of Trade and wife of the editor of the *San Jose Mercury*. Mrs. Laura Watkins, who lived on South Tenth, was manager of the women's exhibits. (McGlincy was to gain national attention three years later on May 26, 1896 when he, his wife, stepson, stepdaughter, maid and ranchhand were cruelly murdered by his crazed son-in-law James C. Dunham. The culprit left the area and was never brought to justice.)

Many local companies, farmers and individuals had their products on view in the Santa Clara County department of the California Building. The J.H. Flickinger Company, one of our first canneries was well represented, as was Paul Masson and his brother-in-law Henry La Franc of Almaden Vineyards. Both received awards for their wines. Other vintners included Paul O. Burns and the Los Gatos-Saratoga Wine Company. Chynoweth and Lion of Edenvale had their peaches on display. Pioneer Moses Schallenberger was represented with jars of loquats in solution. The McGlincys exhibited peaches in solution as well as assorted table fruits.

A number of fruit producing counties had giant displays of their principle product. San Diego had a huge pyramid of boxed raisins. Santa Barbara had a twenty foot tower of cans of olive oil, and Los Angeles County had its "orange globe" made up of 6,280 fresh oranges. Not to be outdone, and certainly the winner of the most imaginative display, was our

county's life size "prune horse and rider" (see photo previous page). The sign below this finely detailed prune figure left no doubt in anyone's mind about the identity of the leader of the prune world: Santa Clara County — 20 million pounds; the rest of the U.S. — 9 million pounds.

Andrew Hill and his partner Sidney York sent an exhibit of their photographs of the Santa Clara Valley. Robert Bulmore, financial agent of the Quicksilver Mining Company had a display on the New Almaden Mines, and the Lick Observatory exhibited a series of transparencies of the "heavenly bodies." C.P. Bailey, proprietor of the Angora Robe and Glove Factory on North Fourth Street, whose angora goats won blue ribbons at other world's fairs, had a display of his angora rugs. Professor Carl Zeus "late of the Royal Academy of Art, Munich," whose studio and residence were in the Farmer's Union Building in San Jose, was represented by some of his watercolors.

A number of local women artists and writers were featured in the Women's Department of the state building. One of the most prominent exhibits was the poetry of Mrs. Carrie Stevens Walter, editor and proprietor of the monthly *Santa Clara*. Betty Tisdale, who resided on The Alameda, Mrs. Mary H. Field who lived on Clifton Place and Molly Taafe also made literary contributions. Miss Ida May Coates, who was to make a name for herself among local artists, won recognition for two paintings: "Ideal Head" and "Greek Girl." The San Jose Eschscholtzia China Painting Club (they met the first Monday evening of the month in the old Porter Building) was represented with sets of their painted chinaware. The lounge in the Women's Department was called the "Eschscholtzia Poppy Room" to honor the man who first identified the blossom that was to become our state flower in 1903.

By this time California was already touting its advanced approach to education, and our county schools, public and parochial, had displays of their teaching materials. Featured, of course, was our own San Jose State Normal, the first and foremost teacher's college in the West.

In 1893 the land west of the Rockies was as unfamiliar to the masses in the East as the dark side of the moon. Californians, justly proud of their achievements in the short time since statehood, needed to sell the rest of the world on the benefits of the state, its climate, agricultural and mineral abun-

dance and its scenic attractions. The World's
Columbian Exhibition was the perfect place to show
off. Some might now lament that we were ultimately
too successful.

The 1907 Thomas-Flyer which won the 1908 New York – Paris Race. From the Illustrated Encyclopedia of the World's Automobiles.

# The Great Race Comes to Town

1908 WAS AN EXCITING YEAR FOR THE GROWING number of automobile enthusiasts in the Santa Clara Valley. It was in the spring of that year that the cars of the great New York to Paris race would pass through San Jose on the first gruelling car race to circle the globe.

Sponsored by the *New York Times* and the Paris newspaper *Le Matin*, this race was to test the endurance of the automobiles and drivers from four countries: France, Germany, Italy and the United States. The French were represented by three autos, a Motobloc, a De Dion and the Sizaire-Naudin. The

Italians drove a Zust, the Germans a Protos and the Americans a Thomas Flyer. Built by the Thomas Motor Company of Buffalo, the Flyer was powered by a 72 hp 6-cylinder engine.

The route of the race, which began February 12th from New York's Times Square, was to Chicago, across the midwest, through Wyoming and Nevada to San Francisco. From San Francisco, cars and drivers were to go by boat to Valdez, Alaska, then drive across the frozen Bering Straits, through Asia and Europe to Paris.

Considering February/March weather and the

fact that at this time there were no paved roads beyond the edges of the major cities, one had to be an optimist to hope that any auto could get across the U.S. let alone around the world. The hilarious film of some years back, (*The Great Race* starring Tony Curtis and Jack Lemmon) was based on this actual contest. The real race was no less bizarre as the four nations competed against each other and almost impossible odds to prove that their respective countries were superior in the dawning mechanical age.

After five weeks of punishing travel with many mishaps, the racers were rumored to be approaching San Jose. The Thomas Flyer had led the race most of the way and was by now 800 miles ahead of the nearest competitor. After stopping to rest for the night in Los Banos, the Americans had to navigate the Pacheco Pass on the following morning without the guidance of a pilot car (pilot cars preceded the racers all along the route to guide the way). Not surprisingly, the Thomas crew lost their way on the pass and were delayed several hours.

Santa Clara Auto Club members stationed themselves all along the route from Gilroy to San Jose to follow the Flyer team to glory. San Joseans were temporarily fooled — according to the *Mercury*: *an amusing incident happened last night when Earl Fancier with a number of other employees of the Osen and Hunter garage rigged up an automobile and tore madly up First Street with buckets, stepladder, pans and a bale of hay dispersed about the machine. Many of the spectators thought at first that the big race was passing and cheered madly.*

When the Thomas Flyer finally arrived at 11 A.M. on Tuesday, March 24th, it circled through downtown to the exaltation of the excited crowds. The driver, crew and officials retired to the La Molle House for an elaborate dinner provided by the Santa Clara County Automobile Club. Among the diners were M.R. Fletcher of the *Denver Post* and his driver who had been following the American car from Colorado, John R. Chace of the the local auto club, Gus Lion, E.L. Tutt, A.E. House, W.F. Hunt whose garage was servicing the race entrants, E.F. Breniger and representatives of the press. Just as the diners were about to start eating, the orchestra began playing the *Star Spangled Banner* and the crowd rose, some waving flags and handkerchiefs.

According to reports in the *Mercury*, Harold Hansen, the leader of the American team, had reser-

## THE LA MOLLE HOUSE

It was only appropriate that all the contestants in the Great Auto Race of 1908 were feted at San Jose's La Molle House. Since 1872, when it was founded by Madame Veuve La Molle, the La Molle House was the town's premiere establishment for continental cuisine. Located in the three-story building on the northeast corner of Santa Clara and San Pedro Streets (a city landmark now housing the El Maghreb Moroccan restaurant) the La Molle House was a gathering place for the French community of San Jose.

Madame La Molle, who studied the art of cooking in France, had practiced her art for 30 years in Nevada. Shortly after the death of her husband Bernard, Madame La Molle, with her son Emile and daughter Marie moved to San Jose. By 1888 their hostelry was serving an average of 75 transient guests per day. The upper floors included 27 sleeping rooms. Emile La Molle, who was born in Nevada in 1859, eventually took over the business from his mother. During his stewardship the La Molle House had a number of famous French chefs in its employ including Mr. Alexis Gaston who had formerly been a chef at the famous Delmonico's in New York City. An advertisement in the 1883 city directory referred to the place as "the Delmonico Restaurant of San Jose." The postcard reprinted on the next page advertised: "High class family cafe — music every Sunday." After serving San Jose's finest for 45 years, the La Molle House closed its doors in 1917.

In 1904, Emile, with several partners from the French community, opened the La Molle Grill at 36 North First Street which served gourmet meals until 1922. The La Molle House and the La Molle Grill were two of the many businesses run by French immigrants which gave early San Jose a cosmopolitan flavor.

vations about whether they would be able to cross the ice between Alaska and Siberia: *We now are too late by at least two weeks. The rivers are by this time beginning to break up and it would be impossible to go that way.* When asked whether he feared the drive across Siberia, he stated: *Not the least. We have already passed through Indiana, the American Siberia, the worst piece of country I ever saw in winter, and when we get to the real Siberia it will be smooth by comparison.*

Hansen also told reporters that the racers were planning to cross parts of Asia on the railroad rails. The cars had devices called "flanges" which allowed them to run on the rails. As Hansen had predicted, the Alaska route was scrubbed and the cars were shipped across from Seattle to Vladivostok.

The seemingly obvious superiority of the American machine and the patriotic implications of an American victory did not dampen the local crowd's enthusiasm for the French and Italian cars which were to follow. When the Italian Zust arrived on April 3rd, the *Mercury* heralded: *A royal reception is given them in San Jose when they reach here ... thousands of residents thronged the road from San Jose to far below the town of Gilroy. Over one hundred joined the Italian crew in an excellent spread at the La Molle House.* The Italians had such a good time that they made an unplanned layover in San Jose.

When the French De Dion arrived (the two other French entries had dropped out) four days later, the French community headed by Albert Ferbos was out in force. To their disappointment, the French team stayed only long enough for a hasty meal at the La Molle House. To the local club La France they gave a lengthy written apology which concluded: *For the first time since we left Paris we have tasted the genuine cuisine francaise and we thank sincerely the able chef Armand Vivier of the La Molle House.*

The local German community was denied the opportunity to welcome their homeland's Protos car for it broke down near Salt Lake City and was transported to Seattle by train. Undaunted, the Protos reentered the race at Vladivostok, and after exchanging the lead several times with the Americans, reached Paris first to claim the prize.

After some deliberation, race officials penalized the Germans for the 1300 miles travelled by train in

*Old postcard of the LaMolle House, "A high class Family Cafe, with Music Every Sunday, at Santa Clara and San Pedro Streets, San Jose, California." From the collection of Jack Douglas.*

the U.S., making the Thomas Flyer the unqualified winner of the New York to Paris race.

San Jose's point on the route of the Great Race gave a real boost to the many local auto enthusiasts, brought solidarity to the several cultural groups, and for a few short weeks, raised the spirits of San Joseans high as they shared in the spectacle of one of the most publicized events of the time.

# San Jose Greets the Great White Fleet

THE NEW YORK TO PARIS AUTO RACE WAS NOT THE only international event to engage the attention of San Joseans in the spring of 1908. They also had the opportunity to see the greatest naval armada of modern times.

President Teddy Roosevelt had decided that it was time to let the world know that the United States was a world power, and to do so he sent the bulk of the U.S. Navy around the world on a "goodwill tour." It was no secret to the British and the Japanese that this unprecedented show of power was to let them know that we were fully capable of protecting our pos-

U.S. Battleship "Illinois". Postcard courtesy of Jack Douglas.

sessions in the Pacific which had been recently acquired during the Spanish-American War.

To make the fleet seem less menacing, Roosevelt insisted (over the objections of his admirals) that the ships be painted white instead of the traditional grey. Since the world would be watching it was essential that there be no mishaps — no collisions at sea or bad behavior by the men when visiting foreign ports. With this in mind, the sailors were recruited from smaller midwestern towns where more "representative" American boys might be expected to live.

Naval power was something new to Americans who had lived in isolation following the Civil War. Although the ironclad was invented during the war, no modern U.S. metal warships were built until the 1890s. The typical American had little knowledge of these mighty warships so the arrival of the whole fleet was much anticipated and proved to be an awesome experience for the folks in California. For Bay Area residents it was an opportunity to show off the results of their rebuilding efforts following the '06 quake.

The route of the fleet was as follows: from New York, around South America, up the West Coast to San Francisco (with a pause for freshening up), on to Australia via Hawaii, then to China and Japan. The homeward journey would take them through the Indian Ocean, the Suez Canal, the Mediterranean and back to New York.

As the fleet steamed up the West Coast many cities along the way vied for the opportunity to host a landing. Monterey was greatly disappointed when the fleet opted instead for Santa Cruz. Mishaps on the first leg of the journey were minor: a rash of the fever; an incapacitating case of rheumatism which struck Admiral Evans (he relinquished his command in San Francisco); and a storm off Santa Cruz during which the battleship *Illinois* (see photo previous page) lost her anchor, drifted some distance and narrowly missed colliding with the *Alabama*.

San Joseans, led by attorney and Chamber of Commerce president Victor Scheller, had planned for months on their contribution to the welcoming of the fleet. The decision was made to transport 300 officers by train to San Jose, give them a luncheon and an auto tour of the valley.

The big event, however, was the grand entrance of the fleet through the Golden Gate. The *San Jose Mercury* reported: *San Jose is deserted when fleet arrived, estimated 10,500 go to watch battleships enter Golden Gate...eighteen trains packed to full capacity with excursionists to San Francisco left the broad gauge depot Wednesday morning.* Banks, schools, businesses and even the library closed for the day. More than 100 automobiles headed north as did motorcycles and bicycles. The Knights of Columbus chartered two ferry boats which took them to a special grandstand atop Telegraph Hill. Members of the South Bay Yacht Club viewed the spectacle from their boats.

The editorial in the *Mercury* summed it up as follows: *All the world loves a pageant...such a spectacular show appeals to all classes of people, from the most gifted and cultivated all the way down to the coarsest, most ignorant and degraded. Those human beings who profess to care nothing for such a pageant are either prigs who are lying about it, or sodden and*

Reprinted from 1970 Number Nine Keepsake Series of the Book Club of California entitled Peace Voyage of the U.S. White Fleet.

abnormal creatures who furnish the exception to prove the rule.

Southern Pacific ran a large ad which exclaimed: *Our armada, greatest ever assembled, forty six monsters move as a unit...see the electrical display at night...visit the ships...greatest military and naval parade ever witnessed. Round trip fare $1.70.*

It seemed as if everyone in northern California was on hand to greet the fleet. A correspondent on one of the ships wrote later in *Harper's Weekly: We wanted to grasp the impulse, just as they had felt it, which had brought them out yonder by the hundred thousands, in human blotches on the steeps...flies like flies. I suppose this simile occurred to half of the 16,000 men. I heard a dozen lips mutter it, from officer down to stokes.*

First through the Gate were the 18 battleships. They were saluted on both sides by the Army forts. Inside the Bay they were joined by the cruisers of the Pacific fleet. All passed in review before the Secretary of Navy who stood on the gunboat *Yorktown*. The ships then anchored in three columns just south of the Ferry Building. A massive naval and military parade was held the next day, May 7th, which served as a prelude to a fortnight's festivities.

On the twelfth, San Jose played host to a some-what sated contingent of naval officers. They arrived at the Bassett Street train station to be greeted by the Fifth Regimental Band, after which they were led to the Vendome and St. James Hotels for lunch. The list of residents who volunteered to chauffeur the officers on the valley tour is a veritable who's who of prominent citizens: Gus Lion, George Polhemus, W.M. Clayton, E.L. Wolfe, Judge J.R. Welch, W.V. Dinsmore, Wilbur Henning, Fred Herold, Mrs. Stella O. Moon, J.O. Hayes, J.H. Rucker, L. Normandin, William Binder, Hugh Center and many others.

A highlight of the tour was the stop at Santa Clara College where they were greeted by the men of the college, young ladies of the Notre Dame Academy and pupils of St. Joseph's Parochial School. After a greeting by Rev. Richard A. Gleeson, Santa Clara's President, a poem was read by student James R. Daly. Each stanza was punctuated by a college yell: "rah! rah! rah! the fleet!" The poem (see text below) seems a perfect reflection of the event and the place.

A surprise awaited the officers upon their return to the train. The engine and cars had been bedecked with masses of floral decorations that had been prepared in an adjacent warehouse. Our hearty sea dogs must have striven mightily to hold back their manly tears when they were overwhelmed with bouquets

---

## WELCOME TO THE CAPTAINS OF THE FLEET

### TUESDAY, MAY 12, 1908

Heirs of heroes with whose glorious deeds our annals are replete,—
Freedom's warriors whose brave story knows nor shame nor base retreat,—
With the warmth of California hearts your noble band we greet!
Welcome thrice and three times o'er from bannered town and shouting street!

From our purple-fruited orchards, from our fields of golden wheat,
From our hills, where the Sequoias guard their kindgom's ancient seat,
Rolls the chorus of our welcomes, while glad hearts the measure beat,
And the roses of our vale are strewn a carpet for your feet!

Ye that on the wave triumphant bear Columbia's standard-sheet;
Ye, our pride in peace, our calm reliance still in battle's heat;
Ye, whom Triton loves — the brave, to whom the land's acclaim is meet—
Santa Clara bids ye hail, and dips her pennant to THE FLEET!

---

from the ladies of the various churches and garden clubs. One young officer was quoted as saying that he definitely planned to come to San Jose to live as soon as he made captain. The *Mercury* printed a number of thank you letters from the grateful (and dutiful) officers for the "delightful day in the country."

The stellar appearance of the Navy was not wasted on the youth of San Jose. The *Mercury* noted: *San Jose lads enlist in Uncle Sam's Navy: recruiting station shows the California youth have "dementia nautica."*

When the fleet sailed away on their ultimately successful tour, every San Josean must have felt less isolated and more a part of an emerging world power. For better or worse, our years of innocence were drawing to a close.

# The Great Bridge Disaster of 1917

W E ALL TAKE THE MANY BRIDGES IN DOWNTOWN for granted as we pass to and fro across them. Most of us don't realize, however, that because our city is bisected by three waterways, the Guadalupe River, Los Gatos Creek and Coyote Creek, early San Joseans had to focus considerable attention on transportation across these obstacles. At that time, when our engineering skills were not so sophisticated, it was common for bridges to be washed out in the winter floods. It was, therefore, a great achievment when, in the 1870s, an iron bridge was built across the Coyote Creek at Santa Clara and 17th Streets.

One of the busiest overpasses in town, the Coyote Bridge was the main link to the farmers, factories, lumberyards and other services in the east valley. Two sets of rails traversed the bridge in order to accommodate the popular Alum Rock Trolley line that carried people to East San Jose and out to the wonders of Alum Rock Park.

The people of San Jose realized just how important the bridge was when it collapsed on Saturday afternoon October 20, 1917. The *Mercury Herald*, in their Sunday edition, exclaimed: *The greatest cata-*

*strophe sustained by San Jose since the earthquake of 1906...* . Weighted down by three heavily laden railroad cars, the forty year old structure snapped with an explosive noise and fell into Coyote Creek. A "goat" switch engine was pushing the cars across the bridge when it went down. Fortunately, A.L. Gerber the engineer put on the engine brakes in time to prevent it from joining the boxcars in the creek. Henry Rich, the conductor, hung on to the ladder of one of the cars and rode it down, coming out unscathed. At first it appeared, incorrectly, that no human injuries were sustained.

Until they heard his cries, no one knew that young Lawrence Foster had chosen that moment to be on the bridge. Fred Saunders, a salesman from the nearby San Jose Lumber Company was the first on the scene to realize that there was someone caught in the debris. According to the inquest report, Foster cried: *Please mister, help me.* When asked if there were others with him, he answered no and then asked his older brother who was now on the scene to bring their father. A Mr. Rose carried the boy to the Saunders car and he was rushed to the nearby Garden City Sanitarium. All attempts by Drs.

*Remains of the Coyote Creek Bridge. San Jose Historical Museum Collections.*

Balknap and Wayland were to no avail and Larry died shortly after midnight of shock engendered by his severely crushed leg and possible internal injuries.

The press gave misleading information regarding young Foster's age and also his activities prior to the accident which has been perpetuated in later histories. According to the *Mercury Herald* the twelve year old Larry was delivering milk on his bicycle when the bridge gave way under him. As Clyde Arbuckle recently remarked, this would have been an odd way to be delivering milk as well as an unlikely hour. The real story, as revealed in the coroner's inquest on file in the San Jose Historical Museum's archives, tells a tale of a dutiful son who was probably typical of many boys of his time.

Larry was one of eight children of Mr. and Mrs. P.S. Foster who lived on the east side of the creek at 525 South Nineteenth Street. Mr. Foster was an employee of the American Dairy located just across the bridge at the corner of Seventeenth and Santa Clara. (Later to become the Borden Creamery which occupied the site until the late 1960s.) Larry was fourteen but may have been small for his age, hence the confusion in the paper. In any case, he often helped his father at the dairy, and on that afternoon had assisted his older brother with a delivery which was done with horse and wagon in those days. He was evidently heading home on foot for dinner when the bridge fell.

As one might imagine, there was a great public outcry. Why were there freight cars on tracks meant only for the Alum Rock Trolley? Why hadn't the City replaced the bridge which had been declared unsafe six years before? More practical types wondered how they were going to get back and forth to work, and others were concerned that the prunes in the boxcars, scheduled to be shipped to the Allies, be salvaged before they became soaked in creek water. A *Mercury Herald* editorial seemed to imply that it was a propitious accident: *had these few freight cars not gone down...one filled with human freight must have done so sooner or later. Indeed two heavily laden automobiles might have broken through this structural fraud and a heavy toll of life... .* The thought that the freight with its 200 tons of dried prunes and sugar beets (four times the maximum load for the bridge) saved the lives of the many must have been little consolation to the family of Larry Foster.

The inquest pitted the railroad against the city administration, the former consisting of Peninsula Railway manager Frank Chapin and his attorneys Louis Oneal and James P. Sex, and the latter, City Attorney Earl Lamb and City Manager Thomas Reed. Reed, a former UC professor and city reformer, was the city's first manager to be installed after years of political "bossism" at City Hall. He didn't need this scandal at a time when he was trying to clean up city government. It didn't help matters to have one of his arch foes, Oneal, representing the railroad.

The newspapers were full of charges and countercharges. Reed said that he wasn't aware that freight cars were moving over the bridge, and that the railway had no franchise to do so. He and G.W. Hunt, the newly installed city engineer, pleaded ignorance of the report made six years before that the bridge was unsafe. Hunt testified that a recent inspection found the structure quite capable of carrying loaded trolleys whose weight did not exceed 45 - 50 tons.

Railroad officials maintained that they had a right to be on the bridge because the city had used the same tracks in 1911 to move gravel over the bridge for street improvements. In his testimony, Reed as much as admitted that he and the City Council had looked the other way when the freight cars used the span. It was, after all, in the interest of east side business and city development that the bridge be so used. *We were never wishful to be too technical in our dealings with the company,* Reed stated, *and even had they been caught hauling freight cars in the city, there could be no punishment. We could only have confiscated their franchises, which no one was anxious to do. The city does not want to cut off its nose to spite its face.* Reed shifted the responsibility by stating: *I should imagine that if people want to do something they know they have no right to do, they would be careful to obey the rules of sound judgement in their operations which the company did not do in running something like 200 tons, almost the maximum weight for a railroad bridge, over a bridge only designed for street traffic.*

The *Mercury Herald* editorial entitled "Mr. Chapin and Mr. Reed" ended with this statement: *We are both glad and regretful that the City Manager takes so lightly the violation of railroad franchises; glad that his attitude has been made clear, and regretful that one holding public office of great responsibility should thus irreverentially esteem those legal safeguards which are supposed to stand between the public and corporation injustice.*

East side residents were not so sparing. After having recently voted to be annexed by San Jose, they were not happy to have their access cut off. Mrs. Mary McCarthy, a leading critic, stated: *We are living here in no man's land and if the council don't give us what we want we may do a little re-electing. We have lost faith in the City Manager and the City Council because they have not a representative here (at the meeting.) I believe Mr. Reed is in Stockton talking about good government.*

Gas and water lines to the East Side were soon repaired but automobile traffic had to be rerouted to the Julian Street bridge, and trolley passengers had to leave the trolley and cross a hastily installed footbridge to resume the journey on the opposite bank.

*Boxcars in Coyote Creek.*
*San Jose Historical Museum Collections.*

Reed rejected the idea of a temporary bridge, finding the $10,000 price tag too costly.

The lead article on the front page of the October 26th *Mercury Herald* read: *Blame not placed for bridge crash, coroner's jury does not fix responsibility for death of L. Foster in verdict.* And so the city and the railroad washed their hands of a staggering example of gross negligence. There is no evidence that the Foster family received anything to compensate them for the loss of their son, something almost inconceivable in our present day litigious society.

The scandal was soon forgotten when the public's attention became totally absorbed in the casualty figures and liberty loan drives of World War I. The new bridge, which took fifteen months to build, was opened for traffic in January 1919. By then, the war had been won, Reed had moved on, and headlines were full of news of the great flu epidemic. Theodore Roosevelt died that month so it was decided to name the new structure the Teddy Roosevelt Bridge. In all due respect to Teddy, it had better been named for Larry Foster.

# The 1918 Flu Epidemic

THE 1918 FLU EPIDEMIC DISRUPTED THE LIVES OF almost every citizen of San Jose. Before it was over a fifth of the population would become ill and 200 would die.

Called a pandemic because of the worldwide implications, this infection, often leading to pneumonia, would be responsible for the deaths of tens of millions of people. Its timing could not have been worse, coming as it did during the final months of World War I. Mass movements of troops and refugees contributed to its rapid spread. Dubbed the "Spanish influenza" (there was a major outbreak in Spain), it spread in three waves during 1918-19. The first, in the spring of 1918, affected Europe but was hardly noticed in the United States. The second and most virulent came in October and caught American health authorities unprepared. It subsided in December but returned in January and February of 1919.

News of the epidemic leaped onto the pages of the *Mercury Herald* on October 9: "Influenza Reaches County." Overnight, 153 cases were reported at nearby Camp Fremont. The paper published a Board of Health bulletin: *Spanish influenza is now epidemic in many eastern cities. San Jose should not be alarmed, but should help prevent the disease, if possible.*

The first deaths were reported the following day. Emile Loustalet, age nineteen, and his brother Leon, age six, were the earliest victims. A third brother was to die later. The flu took its greatest toll among San Jose's immigrant Italian and French populations. The crowded conditions and less than sanitary environs contributed to the spread.

On October 11, the paper announced 185 new cases with five deaths. The Board of Health decreed that all churches and schools be closed. Later, moving pictures houses, the YMCA pool and the library were added to the list. Another not so reassuring health bulletin told the readers to "take precautions, but don't worry."

An influenza command center, under the direc-

*Children's Ward, State Normal School, during Flu Epidemic. San Jose Historical Museum Collections.*

tion of city health officer Dr. W.C. Bailey was set up in the Old Theatre Building on North First. From here various directives were given, and a continual appeal for volunteer nurses was made. Many teachers did nursing duty. The city was divided up into sectors to be patrolled by members of the Women's Army, a group of society matrons whose original purpose was the solicitation of monies during Liberty Loan drives. Every home was investigated for possible cases. There was some hesitation about entering the poorer neighborhoods, so these were ministered to by the younger and pluckier women of the Good Cheer Club. These women were experienced in helping the town's needy, and they soon had volunteer car owners lined up to transport the sick to the hospitals.

Numerous steps were taken to stop the spread of the flu. Streets were washed down regularly, coins were sterilized and paper money was fumigated. Sheriff A.B. Langford told the police to avoid sending anyone to jail whenever possible. New vaccines from the east were administered but later evidence showed that they were of little good.

The severe shortage of hospital beds inspired Morris Dailey, President of the Normal School, to offer to transform part of his school into a convalescent hospital. Under the supervision of Dr. Jay C. Elder, the training school building rooms were quickly transformed into hospital wards for sick children. The home economics faculty and students under Miss Margaret Myers were soon turning theory into practice as they prepared wholesome meals for the sick. The health staff and volunteer faculty and students under the guidance of Elizabeth McFadden ministered to the patients.

A constant flow of beds, linen, clothing and other supplies were donated to keep the operation going. Miss Bessie Cole, English teacher at the high school handled the logistics of acquiring thousands of dollars worth of free food from local businesses. A *Mercury* headline summed up a positive aspect of this crisis: *Service develops San Jose's vision, workers who helped combat epidemic get knowledge of needs of poor.*

The flu forced the closure of many local universities such as Stanford and Cal, but the doughty students at the University of the Pacific (then in San Jose) kept at their studies. To answer criticism of this, the president assured the press that each student's temperature was taken before he or she entered the classroom.

The introduction of the gauze face mask was probably the most talked about innovation in the war on influenza. Although prescribed early on as a sure preventative, people were slow to accept the idea of appearing incognito in public. An influenza bulletin warned: "It's better to look 'funny' than perfectly natural." Officer Jackson, the downtown patrolman, was ordered to cite anyone not wearing a mask. The Sunday *Mercury Herald* of November 3, under a headline entitled: "Guess Who," featured a rogues gallery of photos of prominent locals in their masks. The ladies wore laced trimmed masks and the men assumed jaunty poses.

The accompanying article began: *Mask etiquette hasn't developed to such a point that the ordinary diner knows what to do with his facial covering when he slips into a restaurant, the cafeteria or O'Briens for the meal that he must eat away from home. Mike E. Griffith of the D. A.'s office is the leading exponent of one group of people who are in favor of hanging the mask on the port ear as one goes into action at the table. This custom admittedly has its advantages and is especially recommended for absent-minded men, as it is difficult to forget that the mask is attached to the ear when one goes into the street from the eating place; difficulties with Officer Jackson are thus avoided.*

By late December national health authorities had discovered that communities that didn't require masks had the same percentage of cases of flu as those that did. Local authorities continued to encourage their use however.

The disastrous autumn wave of flu began to subside as the November 11 Armistice Day approached. Crowds began massing for victory parades, parties and community singing. The final wave of infection in January 1919 brought back most of the earlier restrictions, but the elation of the ending of the war seemed to mitigate the suffering and loss.

It is perhaps ironic that a plague which in a short time could bring about such universal sorrow and death could be so quickly forgotten. The so-called "Great War" called on the efforts of many, but the influenza epidemic required a similar sacrifice from the people of San Jose and they rose to the occasion with a spirit and dedication of which one could be proud.

*Opening parade at the 1918 Round-up. Photo courtesy of Jack Douglas.*

# The San Jose Round-up Days, 1915 - 1918

OST OF US HAVE SEEN OR HEARD REFERENCES TO an early San Jose event called the Fiesta de las Rosas, but few of us know about a similarly famous happening known as the "Round-ups." During the period of 1915-18, when San Jose was becoming known as the cowboy capital of the West, the Round-ups drew as many crowds and star performers as Cheyenne's Frontier Days. Talented rodeo performers who appeared included: native American champion rider Jack Sundown, magician of the lariat "Skeeter" Bill Robbins, and black bronc rider Ty Stokes.

The Round-ups were held at Luna Park, an amusement park located on the edge of town at 17th and Berryessa. The park, which had been developed by Lewis Hanchett in order to get riders to use his 17th Street railway, was falling upon hard times, so

it was suggested in 1915 that the ballfield be used for a rodeo, the profits of which would be used to "strengthen and beautify" the shaky Light Tower at Market and Santa Clara Streets. (Alas, the tower collapsed five months later during a rainstorm).

The guiding spirit behind the Round-up Days was Louis Oneal, prominent attorney and Republican kingpin. The "cowboy attorney," as he was called, was raised on a Nevada ranch and now owned his own ranch in the hills above Los Altos. He was a close personal friend of San Francisco mayor James Rolph who owned the adjoining ranch. The world's attention was focused, in 1915, on San Francisco's Pan Pacific Exposition. It may have been Oneal's hope to capture some of the limelight by putting on a wild west show in neighboring San Jose.

The first Luna Park Round-up had all the flavor

of a county fair. The usual park attractions, the scenic railway, old mill, circle swing and old merry-go-round, were augmented for the occasion by duck games, doll booths, a country store, a chicken game, shooting gallery, candy booth, hoop-la-game, a new merry-go-round borrowed from Idora Park in Oakland, and a sandwich and hot dog stand. Alex Hart, the department store owner, personally supervised the "Koverall," a sandpile for the kids in which prizes were hidden. One afternoon was given over to the local grammar and high schools for a big track and field contest.

The Round-ups, held every year on the days around the 4th of July, were officially begun at a ceremony on the old City Hall steps and a large parade through town. Everyone in the county with a riding horse was invited to participate. The automobile, or "machine" as it was called then, was just becoming a regular sight on San Jose streets, and later Round-ups would feature long parades of them.

There was a concern on the part of some animal lovers that livestock used in the rodeo might be hurt. To allay these fears, the Chamber of Commerce passed a rule by which they could "disbar and prosecute riders who drew blood on a horse or bull." Spurs were to be taped so such tender beasts as "Tango Annie," "Glass Eye," "High Tower," and the most notorious bronco of all, "Coyote," would not be unduly marred. No such precautions were taken for the riders.

Looking back, the 1916 Round-up appears to have been the high water mark of all the shows. Starting on July 1 and culminating in a giant 4th of July bash, it seemed to sum up a period of American innocence which was forever swept away by our entry, the following year, into World War I.

Oneal and his committee of wranglers, who included Sheriff A.B. Langford, Joseph DeBraty, Frank Martin, Gus Went,

George Broderick, Dudley Dinsmore and automobile dealer Clarence Letcher, planned a mighty celebration which started at City Hall and spread out as far as St. James Park. To honor the city to the north, the first day of the Round-up was called San Francisco Day, and Mayor Rolph was made honorary parade marshall.

The *Mercury Herald* summed up the activities thusly: *Staid gentlemanly "Jim" Rolph, mayor of San Francisco, who welcomed the world to the Panama Pacific Exposition, came to San Jose yesterday, donned in a gaudy shirt, wooly chaps, a round-up hat and climbed aboard a horse. The next moment he pointed his six shooter at the sky, banged away and let out a cowboy "yip." It was the opening gun for the San Jose Round-up, which will entertain tens of thousands of people from all parts of the state during the next three days. After "shooting up the town"' Mayor Rolph led a colorful parade through the streets of San Jose followed by hundreds of horsemen and horsewomen. In the afternoon a round-up program equalling any ever presented in the west was staged in the magnificent new arena constructed on the old site of Luna Park. At night people were pouring into the city by every train and every road ... San Francisco dispatches said that 10,000 machines started southward on the peninsula toward San Jose during the afternoon and evening. The streets were crowded with people last*

*Fair Riders of the Range at the Round-Up, San Jose 1-2-3-4, 1918. Postcard courtesy of Jack Douglas.*

*night, there was dancing on the streets (bands played all night in Plaza Park and St James Park) and concessionaires did a tremendous business around City Hall. Autos were being parked for the night on many business and residence streets.*

At Round-up Park the proceedings began with the official Round-up song "Girl of My Dreams" sung through a megaphone by its composer James Cushing. There followed a series of rodeo events, including such favorites as the potato race, the Roman race in which riders stood on two galloping steeds, a chariot race, and the ever favorite girl's nightgown race, described by the *Mercury Herald* as: *a bit of comedy ... the entries were required to dash from one end of the track to the other with a closed package containing a nice white nightgown, tucked under one arm, and when on the other side, to leap off the horse, draw the nightgown modestly over their respective heads and, looking very much like belated members of the Ku Klux Klan, go streaming back to the finish line.* The winner was Rose Walker followed by Sallie Ractor and Skeeter Bill's wife Dorothy Morrell. Dorothy, who rode under her maiden name, participated in all the women's events. Although seriously trampled midway during the events, she appeared gamely upon her horse on the final day.

The most unusual event took place on Monday when Miss Ethel Addleman and Mr. Russell Stafford were joined in marriage on horseback on Round-up field in front of God and 20,000 spectators. As the *Mercury* described it: *Theirs will be one of the most spectacular weddings that has been held in California in many years; it being a genuine Round-up ceremony. The bride, groom and clergyman will be mounted on the finest horses to be procured in this county and be attended by 200 cowboys and cowgirls in full costume, mounted upon their horses.*

Meanwhile, back at City Hall a stunt man called "The Human Fly" was entertaining the crowds by sliding head first down a cable attached to the top of City Hall and strung south to San

Carlos Street. At night this event was illuminated by colored lights According to the *Mercury* reporter, *the effect being that of a couple of comets coursing through the darkness.*

One of the days was designated "Homecoming Day," and all former citizens of the city were welcomed back by a committee of San Jose's elite to a grand reception at the Courthouse.

Fourth of July pageantry gave an added dimension to the last day of the Round-up. Principal speakers at the City Hall ceremonies included the newly appointed city manager, Thomas Reed. The

Stunt Rider. Photo courtesy of Jack Douglas.

Governor, Hiram Johnson, had been invited but sent as his deputy, John F. Neylan, President of the Board of Control. Under the leadership of Professor F.F. Jeffers, the boy's glee club sang stirring renderings of "We'll Never Let the Old Flag Fall" and "The Old Flag Has Never Touched the Ground." The opening parade led by a crack marching group called the California Grays included marching groups from all the fraternal and military groups in the county. For a nation on the verge of the "Great War;" such patriotic celebration must have seemed quite appropriate.

Not all of the Round-up visitors came for the patriotic speeches. According to Clyde Arbuckle, sporting women were drawn to the Round-ups from all over to satisfy the lusty cowboys and their followers, and the bawdy houses on Post and San Pedro Streets had long waiting lines.

The good citizens of San Jose must have had a giant collective hangover when they awakened on Wednesday morning the fifth. Never had such an extended party with such hordes of out-of-towners been attempted in the then small town.

The Round-ups during the war years were more subdued. Advertisements announced that all proceeds would be for the benefit of the soldiers, so perhaps the celebration became more of a duty than a pleasure. In 1917 a grand non-sectarian religious gathering was held on Sunday featuring opera diva Bernice de Pasquale. The 1918 Round-up featured Dustin Farnum, star of numerous silent cowboy films. This final Round-up featured one of the best lineups of rodeo performers ever seen, but the enthusiasm had waned.

After the war, innocent joys were supplanted by the cynicism of the 20s. The image of San Jose as a frontier town was soon forgotten. As a sign of things to come, Luna/Round-up Park was sold to developers who turned the area into what was probably our first industrial park.

# Renzel, Politics and Progress

TWO DECADES OF MACHINE POLITICS IN SAN JOSE were abruptly ended in the spring of 1944 when Ernest Renzel and the five other candidates of the Progress Committee were swept into office.

San Jose had seen considerable growth in the period between the wars, but there had been no growth in the basic city services such as fire and police protection, sewers, sanitation, parks and airport facilities. City government was controlled by Charlie Bigley who ran a string of businesses, licit and illicit, which flourished under his patronage at City Hall. Charlie could get out the votes for his candidates for City Council, and as long as he had at least four of the seven Council seats beholden to him he could effectively control the city manager and any other departmental appointments including the superintendent of schools.

The citizens of San Jose thought that they had defeated machine politics when they approved the new city charter in 1915. The charter eliminated the position of mayor and put control of city government in the hands of a council appointed city manager. Thomas Reed, a Berkeley scholar who later became a national authority on city planning, set the new system in motion. He soon left and was succeeded briefly by Willard Bailey.

Then in 1920 city engineer Clarence Goodwin took up the reins and held them for the next 24 years. A Presbyterian elder and conservative administrator, Goodwin ran a tight ship that didn't require new taxes. He was a survivor, and in order to keep his job he had to pay close attention to the desires of the man who had the votes on the City Council: Charlie Bigley.

Charlie Bigley was a San Jose phenomenon — a rags to riches success story. Forced to begin earning his living at the age of 12, he became a hustler on the streets of San Jose in the 1890s. As a driver for a local bakery he made friends all over town. He soon became a popular figure in the ethnic and working class neighborhoods, passing out favors and introducing immigrants to the unfamiliar political system. His first business was a cigar store across from the train station on Bassett Street. Realizing that the automobile was the ticket to the future, he started a taxi fleet from the train station which led in turn to car rentals for funerals, automobile maintenance and storage and an ambulance service.

When prohibition was abolished in 1933 Charlie was first on the street as partner and distributor for the Tacoma Brewing Company. He also owned illegal slot machines and was rumored to be involved in other local gambling enterprises. In order for his businesses to function smoothly he needed the cooperation of the police department, so city manager Goodwin didn't interfere with Bigley's assignments of jobs in the police and fire departments. Everyone knew that if you wanted to be a cop or fireman you went to Charlie Bigley whose office was conveniently located in his garage across Market Street from the old city hall. Former chief Ray Blackmore got his start on the force, in spite of the fact that he didn't meet the height requirements, because Bigley felt that he would be an asset to the department's baseball team. Out of loyalty to their mentor, the boys in police and fire could always be counted on to get out the vote for Charlie's candidates for City Council.

Seats on the City Council rotated so that one, or at the most two, candidates ran on any election year, allowing Bigley to focus on getting out the vote for his candidate. Since there were never controversial issues on the ballot — taxes, city bonds, etc.— the attendance at the polls was usually light, making it easy for Bigley to swing the votes in favor of his men. Bigley's candidates for Council were invariably small businessmen who found that their enterprises improved with orders for products and services from City Hall and the police and fire departments.

By big city standards San Jose "bossism" was pretty benign. Bigley had no grandiose visions or power or greed. He was a big-hearted man, fond of children and difficult to dislike, but he used the democratic system to gratify his own ends at the expense of the general welfare.

Attempts at reform were made in the late 1930s. The youthful Clark Bradley made some inroads during his term on the Council by placing an amendment to the city charter on the ballot that created a San Jose Unified School District independent of City Hall. But he could never break the Bigley block on the Council when it came to replacing Clarence Goodwin.

With the coming of the second world war it became apparent that small town bossism and the status quo would have to end. San Jose was ripe for progress. Bigley's bubble burst in 1944 when, due to council members retiring or joining the armed services, six of the seven council seats became vacant at once.

The younger generation, tired of Bigley's lock on the city, formed the San Jose Progress Committee. The *San Jose Mercury* announced: *San Jose Progress Committee intends to draft the top men in the community to become candidates for City Council.* Specifications for their candidates would be:

1. Unquestioned integrity and intellectual honesty
2. Possession of managerial ability and good common sense
3. Complete absence of prejudice or bias against any group or class of society in the community

The committee pledged to seek no pre-election pledges or make no post-election demands upon the candidates.

The committee selected six of its members to run for City Council. They included: Ernest Renzel, wholesale grocer; Roy Rundel, neon sign manufacturer; Fred Watson, mechanic and labor leader; James Lively, dried fruit packer; Benjamin Carter, FMC comptroller; and Albert J. Ruffo, attorney. Ruffo remembers the situation thus: *Fred Watson was willing to run for office but none of the other five persons were willing... After arguments by several members of the committee... and strenuous arm-twisting, one by*

*one, each nominee surrendered as long as all the others so selected would also run.*

The six candidates were to run on the Progress platform. They would share the campaign expenses and emphasize the fact that a vote for one would be a vote for all. What ensued would be one of the hottest elections seen in sleepy San Jose in over 50 years. Newspaper ads by the Progress candidates stressed

Original campaign materials provided courtesy of Ernie Renzel.

## Here's Your Balanced Council!

Fred Watson    James W. Lively    Albert J. Ruffo

Roy H. Rundle    Ernest H. Renzel, Jr.    Ben C. Carter

*Courtesy of Ernie Renzel.*

an end to bossism, the town's inadequate fire equipment, the need for a better sewer system, more parks and streamlined city services. The Bigley candidates stressed their past effectiveness in city management, citing low crime rates and an "excellent" record in fire protection.

The newspapers predicted a close race, but a record number of voters turned out to elect the Progress candidates by a 2 to 1 majority. All of the members of the Progress slate received over 10,000 votes. Ernest Renzel, who appeared twice on the ballot, once to fill an unexpired term and once again for another four years, was the top vote getter with 11,701 for the unexpired term and 13,702 for the four

year term. Looking for all the world like the Jimmy Stewart character out of Frank Capra's film *Mr. Smith Goes to Washington,* Renzel became Council president.

Mr. Renzel has told this writer that the Progress councilmen had no immediate specific agenda, but the disastrous fire at Garden City Pottery only a week after they took office forced an issue. The fire exposed gross mismanagement on the part of both police and fire departments and exhibited how old and inadequate the city's fire equipment was. Twenty-five years of Bigley control and Goodwin austerity had come home to roost.

Renzel and the new Council ordered that Goodwin retire the veteran police and fire chiefs.

Police chief John N. Black had been on the force since 1902 and fire chief Charles Plummer had seen 30 years of service. Loyal to his chiefs, Goodwin implied that he was retiring them under duress. This so incensed Renzel and the other Councilmen that they demanded Goodwin's resignation. John Lynch, veteran city clerk, was appointed acting city manager. He was the tough new broom, says Renzel, that would sweep through the slack city departments. After years of quietly observing how the city was run, Lynch knew exactly where to turn on the heat.

He appointed William Brown to head the police department. A number of officers were fired, retired and demoted, and the newspapers reported a crackdown on illegal gambling and slot machines. Fire Captain Lester O'Brien was promoted over more senior officials to become the new fire chief.

The Progress Council came to power at a pivotal period in the city's history. Shortly after the election the war ended and the wartime ban on construction and development also ended. Thousands of servicemen were choosing California as a place to work and raise families. San Jose needed progress with a capital P. It came slowly at first. Of five bond issues to improve the city infrastructure, only the one to separate the sewer and storm drain system got the necessary two-thirds vote. Parking meters were installed downtown. Plans were made for emergency housing for servicemen and for an expanded airport, a new city hall, and new industries.

Not forgetting the past, Ernest Renzel proposed the formation of the Historic Landmarks Commission.

At the end of his term as Council president, Renzel moved that the Council give succeeding presidents the title of Mayor, starting a process that has led us back to an elected chief executive.

Some might lament the passing of the good old days when all you needed to get a permit or a ticket fixed was a nod from Charlie Bigley, but San Jose was destined to grow, and it demanded leaders who could plan for the future. The voters, in their wisdom, knew what they were doing when they elected the Progress candidates. We should tip our hats to Rundel, Lively, Watson, Carter, Ruffo and Renzel for taking time from their families and businesses to set the city on a new course. The last three are still living and enjoying their retirement.

# Index

Adams Street, 63
Adele, Marie, 72
Aesthetic Movement, 47
Agnews State Hospital, 93
Aladdin Studio, 32
Alger, Horatio, 89
Alice Building, 17
Almaden College, 105
Almaden University, 105
Almaden Vineyards, 71-72, 119
Almaden Winery, 71-73
Alum Rock Log Cabin, 59-60
Alum Rock Mineral Springs Hotel, 107
Alum Rock Park, 5, 59-60, 107, 116, 129
Alum Rock Park Log Cabin, 59-60
Alum Rock Trolley, 12, 129-130
Amenhotep Shrine, 116
American Dairy, 130
American Grill, 115
American Theater, 45
Amigos Club Quartet, 86
Amtrak, 85
Anderson, Dorothy, 83
Anderson, Dr., 108
Annie, Tango, 136
Anthony, Susan B., 12
Arbuckle, Clyde, 2, 111, 130, 137
Arbuckle, Fatty, 35-36
Arion Press, 4
Art Deco, 79, 81-82
Aspen West Corporation, 79
Atherton, Gertrude, 20
Auditorium Theatre, 32
Audley Ingersoll Amusement Company, 58
Axle Corporation, 58
Azule, 107
Baggerly, Hiland, 30
Bailey, C. P., 119
Bailey, Dr. W. C., 134
Bailey, Willard, 139
Baird, Spencer Fullerton, 2
Bancroft Library, 4, 17, 29
Bank of Italy, 75, 80
Bank of San Jose, 11
Bannister, Reverend Edward, 51
Bay Bridge, 80
Beans, T. Ellard, 11, 99
Beasley, Judge W. A., 60
Beatty, James, 37
Belasco, David, 36

Beldon, Judge, 9-10
Belknap, Dr. Lewis, 62
Belknap Sanitarium, 62
Bellarmine College Preparatory, 51
Benicia, 50
Bennett, Ann, 104
Benoist, Louis, 73
Benson, Victor, 41
Bernal Rancho, 14
Berryessa, 58, 135
Bierce, Ambrose, 5
Bierstadt, Albert, 110
Bigley, Charlie, 139, 142
Binder, William, 39, 43, 45-46, 91, 127
*Bird of Paradise*, 32
Bischoff's Surgical Supply, 80
Bishop, Charles, 86
Black, Jack, 32-34
Black, John N., 142
Blackmore, Ray, 139
Blanche, Ari Lorenz, 34
Bland, Henry Meade, 20
Blodgett Springs, 107
Bohemia Cafe, 115
Bohemian Club, 20, 100
Book Club of California, 126
Borcher Brothers, 75
Borden Creamery, 130
Boston, Robert, 106
Bow, Clara, 36
Bradfield, Max, 40
Bradley, Clark, 140
Broderick, George, 136
Brohaska, Tillie, 60
Brohaska Orchestra, 60
Brown, A. Page, 17, 96, 101, 118
Brown, William, 17, 27, 142
Browning, Sarah Louise, 11
Bruce, Eddie, 83
Bryan, William Jennings, 102
Budd, James, 102
Bulmore, Robert, 119
Burbank Theater, 42
Burnham, Daniel, 19
Burns, Paul O., 119
Burrell, F. L., 75
Burrell Building, 44
Burton, J., 89
Butman, Frederick, 110
Cabrillo, Juan Rodriguez, 19
Cahill, Hiram, 86
Cahill Station, 85-86
California Building, 17, 19, 43-44, 117, 119
California Fox Theatre, 37, 41, 76

California Grays, 137
California Pioneer, 11, 60
California Theatre, 37, 41, 47, 75-76
CalTrain, 85
Cambiano Art Fixtures, 26
Camera Cinemas, 41
Camera Three, 35
Camp Almaden, 105-106
Camp Fremont, 133
Camp Mt. Madonna, 105-106
Camp Rancho Solis, 106
Campbell Fruit Growers Union, 119
Campbell High School, 26
Campen, Fritz, 82
Cannery Row, 27
Cantor, Eddie, 34
Capitol Theatre, 34
Capra, Frank, 141
Carlota, Empress, 4
Carmichael, Mamie P., 60
Carnegie, Andrew, 63, 88-89
Carnegie Library Building, 44, 88, 91
Carter, Benjamin, 140
Castle, N. H., 99
CCC, 105-106
Cedar Brook Park, 57
Chaboya, Antonio, 65
Chace, John R., 122
Chamber of Commerce, 86, 106, 126, 136
Chapin, Frank, 131
Christian Assembly Church, 46
Christian Science Church, 24
Christie, J. H., 86
Chubb, Vivian, 28
Chynoweth, T. B., 14-15
City Market Hall, 111
Civic Auditorium, 45, 75, 91, 115
Civilian Conservation Corps, viii, 105-106
Clayton, W. M., 127
Clayton, W. S., 82
Coates, Ida May, 119
College of Notre Dame, 51, 87, 127
College Park, 52-55, 91
College Park Station, 52
Collegiate Institute, 51
Collins, William, 9-10
Commercial Building, 44-45
Commercial Club, 45
Congress Springs, 107-108
Conway, Will R., 82
Cooper, Astley D. M., 63, 112
Cooper Medical College, 23
Coxhead, Ernest, 50
Coyote Creek, 57, 61-63, 111, 129-131

Coyote Creek Bridge, 130
Crane, Walter, 47
Craven, Margaret, 77
Crest Theatre, 36-37
Cribari Winery, 69
Crocker Museum, 109-110
Cunan, R., 62
Cupertino, 29
Curtis, E. N., 91
Curtis, F. A., 91
Cushing, James, 137
D. B. Cooper Saloon, 72
Dailey, Morris, 55, 134
Daly, James R., 127
Day, W. P., 76
De Anza Hotel, 77, 79, 81-84, 86
De Dion, 121, 123
DeBraty, Joseph, 136
Deichman, O. A., 42
Del Monte Hotel, 14, 88
Delmas, D. M., 9
Deluxe Theater, 38-40, 44
Derby, Charles, 31
Dinsmore, Dudley, 136
Dinsmore, W. V., 127
Diridon, Rod, 85
Doerr, Fred, 75, 82
Donner Party, 1, 30, 110
Doremus, 96
Duke, Wilbur, 106
Dunham, James C., 119
Eagle Brewery, 75
Eagles Hall, 96-97
East San Jose, 21, 61-64, 91, 129
Edenvale, 13-16, 96, 119
Edouart, Alexander, 110-111
Edwin Markham Poetry Society, 20
El Pajaro, 83
El Potrero, 52
Elder, Dr. Jay C., 134
Elks Building, 44
Elks Lodge, 91, 104
Elmwood Jail, 93
Empire Street, 58
Englishtown, 105-106
Enrequita Mine, 110-111
Eschscholtzia China Painting Club, 119
*Esther Damon*, 29
Evergreen, 65-67
Evergreen School, 66
Fairmont Hotel, 75
Fancier, Earl, 122
Farnum, Dustin, 138
Ferbos, Albert, 123

Ferry Building, 96, 101, 127
Fichtner, George, 102
Field, A. G., 99
Field, Arthur, 99
Field, Mary H., 119
Fifth Regimental Band, 91, 127
First Church of Christ Scientist, 96
First National Bank, 85
First Unitarian Church, 96
First Western Bank, 40
Fisher, Thomas, 83
Flickinger Company, 119
Flu Epidemic, viii, 132-134
FMC, 140
Folsom, Mary, 13-14
Forbes, George, 106
Fort Monroe, 105
Fort Ord, 27
Foster, Larry, 130, 132
Foster, P. S., 130
Four Wheel Brake Garage, 103
Fox, Theron, 28, 35, 104
Fox California, 37, 40-41, 45, 76
Fox Mission, 36-37, 40
Fox Padre, 37
Franc, Charles Le, 71-73
Franc, Louise Le, 72-73
Franciscan Ware, 26
Free, Arthur M., 22
Freeman, Frank, 21
Frontier Village, 14, 58
Garden City Bank Building, 44-45
Garden City Pottery, 26, 141
Garden City Sanitarium, 62, 129
Gates, Dr. Howard B., 12, 23-24
Gates Sanitarium, 23
Gates-Maybeck House, 23
Gay Theatre, 38
Georgetown, 110
Gerber, A. L., 129
Germania Hall, 55-56
Gilroy Hot Springs, 106-108
Gladding and McBean, 25-26
Golden Gate Bridge, 106
Good Cheer Club, 134
Goodrich, Levi, 11-12, 96
Goodwin, Clarence, 139-140
Goucher College, 53
Goulet, Oliver, 73
Grant School, 66
Grapes of Wrath, 27-28
Grauman, Sid, 36, 39
Grayson, Andrew Jackson, 1, 3, 109-111
Grayson, Frances, 2, 4

Great Depression, 40, 43, 75, 82, 105
Great White Fleet, viii, 125-128
Greenwood, Charlotte, 34
Griffith, Mike E., 134
Guadalupe River Park, 57
Guinness, Alec, 41
Guth, William Wesley, 53
Guth Hall, 51, 53-54
Hahn, William, 110
Hale, O. H., 90
Hall of Justice, 44
Hammond, John W., 95
Hanchett, Lewis E., 58
Hanchett Park, 41, 49
Hanchett Santa Clara Railroad Company, 57
Hanks, Emily, 8-10
Hanson, Howard, 53
Happy Hollow, 57
Harmon, Charles H., 112
Hart, Alex, 82, 86, 136
Hatch, F. L., 21
Hayes, Anson, 14
Hayes, Everis, 13, 82
Hayes, J. O., 127
Hayes, Rutherford B., 14
Hayes Mansion, 14-16, 96
Hayes-Chynoweth, Mary, 13-16
Hayward, Charlie, 40
Hearst, Phoebe, 23
Hearst, William Randolph, 31
Hedley Lounge, 83-84
Heering, J. H., 96
Henning, Carol, 27-28
Henning, Wilbur, 27, 127
Herold, Fred, 127
Herrmann, A. T., 61
Herrold, Dr. Charles, 44
Hester Theatre, 41
Highland Vineyards, 68
Hill, Andrew P., 1, 112, 119
Hill, Thomas, 110
Hilltop Club, 50
Hippodrome, 37-38
Holmes, Arthur, 103
Homestead Association, 61
Hot Springs Hotel, 108
House, A. E., 122
Houston, James D., 102
Hoyem, Andrew, 4
Hunkins, Stephen B., 55
Hunt, G. W., 131
Hunt, W. F., 122
Hunt, William, 103
Industrial City, 58

Ingalsbe, A.W., 99
Inspiration Point, 105-106
Isabel Island, 4
Jacques, Gideon, 112
Japan, 108, 126
Jeffers, F. F., 137
Jewett, William S., 2, 109-110
John Steinbeck Research Center, viii, 28
Johnson, Hiram, 22, 102, 137
Johnston, Eric, 80
Jolson, Al, 36
Jones, Charles M., 73
Jordan, David Starr, 55
Jose Theater, 38-41, 44
Julian Street, 131
Junior Chamber of Commerce, 106
Keast, Hilda, 83
Keith, William, 17, 110, 112
Kelley Park, 38
Kessler, Friedolin, 105-106
Key, John Ross, 111
Keyes Street, 57
King, F. Loui, 52, 55-56
King, Frank G., 56
King Conservatory, 52, 55-56
King Road, 61, 63
Kiwanis, 77
Knights of Columbus, 75, 126
Knights of the Royal Arch, 62-63
Knox, Virginia, 11
Knox, William, 11
Knox Block, 11
Knox-Goodrich, 11-12
Knox-Goodrich, Sarah, 11-12
Kostka Hall, 51, 54
La Cantina, 83
La France, 123
La Molle Grille, 122
La Molle House, 122-123
Lake Monahan, 57
Lamb, Earl, 131
Langford, A. B., 134, 136
Larkin, Paul G., 26
Le Deit, Sylvan Sr., 94
Lean, W. C., 75
Lee, Don, 26
Leland Stanford University, 52
Lemmon, Jack, 122
Lendrum Tract, 62
Lenzen, Jacob, 63
Lenzen, Theodore, 60
Letcher, Clarence, 97, 103-104, 136
Letcher, George Truman, 103
Letcher, Helen, 103-104

Letcher Garage, 97, 103-104
Levenson, Amelia, 23
Levine, Mort, 31
Lewis, Betty, 91
Lewis, Edmonia, 111
Lewis, Ted, 40
Liberty Grille, 115
Liberty Loan, 132, 134
Liberty Theater, 37-38
Lick, James, 67
Lick Observatory, 60, 115-116, 119
Light Tower, 135
Lima, James B., 42
Lin, Stephen, 77
Lincoln Avenue, 41-42
Lion, Ernest, 76
Lion, Gus, 122, 127
Lion, L., 82, 122
Lions, 57-58, 77
Live Oak Park, 57
Lively, James, 140
Loma Azules, 68
Lonesome Pine, 108
Los Gatos, 28, 57, 129
Los Gatos Creek, 57, 129
Los Gatos-Saratoga Wine Company, 119
Louise Building, 17
Loustalet, Emile, 133
Lumina Theater, 37
Luna Park, 57-58, 135-136, 138
Lyman, Charles S., 95
Lyman, Chester S., 87
Lynch, John, 142
Lyric Theatre, 38
MacMurray, Fred, 83
Madonna of Monterey, 31-32, 34
Madrone Hot Springs, 108
Margaret Pratt Home, 93
Margason, Omar, 105
Marin County, 1
Marine World, 58
Mark Hopkins Hotel, 26, 76
Market Street, 35, 39, 42, 85, 97, 115, 139
Markham, Edwin, 20, 115
Markham Poetry Society, 20
Martin, Frank, 136
Masson, Paul, 71-73, 119
Mathews, Lucia, 50
Matin, Le, 121
Maximilian, Emperor, 4
Maybeck, Bernard, 23-24, 50
Mayfair Theater, 42
McCabe, Jay, 76
McCarthy, Mary, 131

McCarty, John, 68
McClellen, George, 8
McDonald, Angus, 86
McDonald, W. J., 108
McFadden, Elizabeth, 134
McGlincy, P., 119
McKaig, Reverend Dr. W. W., 12
McKee Road, 63
McKinley, President, 102
McLaren, John, 31
McLean, Dan, 37
McNaught, John, 119
McRuer, Helen, 32-34
Medico-Dental Building, 79-80
Mercantile Library, 2
Mercantile Trust Company, 75
Mercury, 9, 13-14, 34, 39, 41-42, 47-48, 58, 62-63, 77, 79-80,
        82-83, 85, 87, 93, 103-106, 111, 119, 122-123, 126,
        128-131, 133-134, 136-137, 140
Mercury Herald, 39, 41, 77, 79-80, 103-105, 129-131, 133-
        134, 136-137
Metcalf, Maurice, 83
Methodist Church, 51
Mexican War, 1, 5
Mexico Theater, 42
Mid-peninsula Open Space District, 31
Mineral Springs, 107-108
Mirassou Winery, 69
Mission School, 2, 51
Mission Theater, 40, 44
Mobedshahi Group, 78
Mohongo, U.S.S., 4
Molle, Emile La, 122
Monahan, Mayor Thomas, 57
Monroe, James, 8
Monterey Road, 57
Montgomery, Shirlie, 83
Montgomery, T. S., 43-45, 55, 75-76, 91
Montgomery Hotel, 39, 45, 76
Moon, Frank H., 62
Moon, Stella O., 127
Moore, Belle, 94
Moore, Judge John Henley, 111
Morgan, Julia, 26, 50
Morgan Hill, 99
Morosco Grand Opera, 36
Morrell, Dorothy, 137
Morris, William, 47, 49
Moszkowski, Moritz, 55
Motobloc, 121
Mt. Hamilton, 104, 106, 115
Mt. Madonna, 105-106
Mt. Madonna Miner, 105-106
Muller, Kathy, viii

Municipal Rose Garden, 31, 116
Murphy Building, 60
Myers, Dr. Gerald, 80
Naglee, Henry M., 5-10, 48, 111
Naglee Brandy, 5, 48, 103, 115
Naglee Monument, 8
Naglee Park, 5, 27, 49, 63, 85, 103
Nahl, Charles Christian, 110
Napa College, 52
Native Daughters, 60
Nevin, Ethelbert, 40
New Almaden, 105-107, 110-111, 115-116, 119
New College, viii, 23
New York Exchange, 17
Newcomb, S. J., 76
Newcomb, William A., 76
Neylan, John F., 137
Normandin, Louis, 82, 127
Notre Dame Academy, 127
Novitiate, 73
O' Briens, 134
O' Connor, Myles P., 111
Oak Hill Cemetery, 12, 24, 45, 57, 86
Oakland Theatre, 76
Oasis Night Club, 97, 103
Occidental Hotel, 10
O' Donnell's Gardens, 57-58
Of Mice and Men, 27
Older, Cora Baggerly, 29
Older, Fremont, 18, 29, 31-33, 116
Olmsted, Frederick Law, 95
Olson, Mother, 46
Oneal, Duncan, 102
Oneal, Louis, 21, 85, 103-104, 131, 135
Optimists, 77
Oracle of Broadway, 32-33
Osen, George, 103
Otis, Elizabeth, 27
Owen, Francis, 37
Owen, J.J., 9, 85
Pacheco Pass, 106, 122
Pacific Congress Springs, 107-108
Pacific Conservatory of Music, 52, 54
Pacific Hotel, 112
Pacific Union Club, 100
Padre Theatre, 37
Page, G. W., 43, 96
Palace of Fine Arts, 24
Palm Haven, 86
Pan Pacific Exposition, 24, 135
Paris Exposition, 25
Paseo Building, 39, 80
Pater, Walter, 47
Patton, Joseph R., 91

Paul Masson Winery, 71, 73
Peninsula Railway, 131
Pepper, Robert D., 48
Perham, Connie, 106
Permian, Helen, 103
Peterson, P. Victor, 94
Petit Trianon, 46
Phelan, James, Sr., 17
Phelan, James Duval, 17, 119
Phelan Building, 31, 101
Phelan Library Project, 20
Pickford, Mary, 40
Pierce, Dr. Robert E., 100
Pinnacles, 105
Place, Clifton, 119
Plaza Park, 90-91, 137
Plummer, Charles, 142
Polhemus, George, 127
Political Equality Club, 118
Polk, Willis, 50, 68, 97
Pope, Ernest, 106
Porter Building, 21, 23, 119
Post Office Building, 90-91, 98
Post St., 25, 101
Poxon, George J., 26
Pratt, Margaret, 93
Pratt, W. W., 93
Pratt Home, 93-94
Prevost, Louis, 57
Price, Caroline, 40
Price, Fannie M., 87
Progress Council, 142
Promised Land, 2, 109-110
Protos, 121, 123
Prune Horse, 118-119
Pussycat Theater, 38
Ractor, Sallie, 137
Ralston Estate, 82
Rambeau, Marjorie, 34
Rancho Villa Vista, 69
Rancho Yerba Buena, 65, 68
Reed, E. C., 99
Reed, James Frazier, 87
Reed, Thomas, 131, 137, 139
Renzel, Ernest, 28, 139-142
Rich, Henry, 129
Richardson, D., 21
Richmond, Harry, 83
Ricketts, Ed, 27
Ringgold, George, 6
Ringgold, Marie Antoinette, 8
Robbins, Bill, 135
Robinson, J. M., 62
Rolph, James, 135

Roop, George, 108
Roosevelt, Eleanor, 83, 106
Roosevelt, Franklin D., 105
Roosevelt, Teddy, viii, 125, 132
Rose Society, 31
Rosegarden, 41, 49
Rosicrucian Park, 116
Round-up Days, 135-138
Rucker, J. H., 127
Rucker, Sam, 99
Rucker Building, 17, 99, 101
Rudolph, L. C., 86
Ruffo, Albert J., 140
Ruggles, Charles, 34
Rundel, Roy, 140
Ruskin, John, 47
Sage, Lewis P., 108
Sage, Louis, 21
Saint James Hotel, 104
Sainte Claire Building, 25, 31, 45, 100
Sainte Claire Club, 18, 31, 73, 96, 99-102
Sainte Claire Hotel, 25-26, 45, 75-78, 100
Sakata, H.K., 108
San Antonio Street, 39, 63, 88
San Benito County, 71
San Carlos Street, 39, 57, 87
San Fernando Street, 87
San Francisco Bulletin, 18, 29
San Francisco Call, 31
San Francisco Chronicle, 28
San Jose Academy, 51
San Jose Athletic Club, 97
San Jose Board of Trade, 119
San Jose Carnegie Library, 63-64, 89-92
San Jose Clinical Laboratory, 80
San Jose Herald, 9
San Jose High School, 27, 88
San Jose Historical Landmarks Commission, viii
San Jose Historical Museum, viii, 13, 20, 30, 35, 38, 57,
        61-62, 64, 85, 96, 104, 112, 114, 130-131
San Jose Hospital, 23, 45
San Jose Institute, 23
San Jose Lumber Company, 129
San Jose Mercury, 13-14, 62-63, 87, 111, 119, 126, 128, 140
San Jose News, 13, 29, 75
San Jose Post Office Building, 98
San Jose Progress Committee, 140
San Jose Public Library, 111
San Jose Railroad, 85, 88
San Jose State Normal School, 25, 85, 87
San Jose State University, 3-4, 6, 21, 25-28, 85, 87-88
San Jose Unified School District, 140
San Jose Weekly, 111
San Juan Bautista, 29-30

Sandburg, Carl, 31
Santa Clara Bar Association, 22
Santa Clara County Automobile Club, 122
Santa Clara County Courthouse, 96
Santa Clara Mission School, 2, 51
Santa Clara Railroad, 57-58, 132
Santa Clara Street, 30, 39, 42, 51, 57, 62-63, 72, 81-82, 86, 137
Santry, Henry, 40
Saratoga Capital, 84
Saunders, Fred, 129
Schaaf, D. L., 62
Schallenberger, Moses, 119
Schell, Mary, 5-6, 8
Scheller, Victor, 126
Schemmel, Frank, 25-26
Schiely, Catherine, 65
Schoonmaker, Frank, 73
Schuetzen Park, 57
Scott, Cora, 13
Scott, Walter, 40
Scottish Rite Temple, 97
Serpa, William, 82
Sex, James P., 131
Shaw, Mason, 41
Sheltering Arms Society, 93-94
Silver Creek, 66
Sisters of Notre Dame, 82, 111
Sizaire-Naudin, 121
Smelzer, Gordon, 64
Smith, E. O., 118
Smith, Frank, 65-66
Smith, Kate, 66
Smith Brothers Store, 65
Smith Creek, 66, 106
Socialist, 29
Solon, Albert, 25-26, 76
Soroptimists, 77
South Bay Yacht Club, 126
South Pacific Railroad, 85
Southern Pacific, 52, 58, 85-86, 108, 115, 127
Southern Pacific Depot, 86
Southern Pacific Station, 86, 115
Spencer, Dr. A. J., 10
Spreckles, Rudolph, 29
Springfield Republican, 113
St. Ignatius College, 17
St. James Hotel, 44, 98
St. James Park, 8, 10, 95-96, 101-103, 115, 136-137
St. James Square Historical District, 95-98
Stafford, Russell, 137
Stanford University, 12, 52, 55
Stanley Steamer, 108
Stanton, Elizabeth Cady, 12

State Theatre, 37
Steinbeck, Carol, 28
Steinbeck, John, viii, 27-28
Steinbeck Research Center, viii, 28
Stephens, Lorenzo Dow, 60
Stickley, Gustav, 50
Stock, Frank, 72
Stockton Ranch, 52
Stokes, Ty, 135
Stone, Lois C., 4
Streets, Margaret, 93
Studio Theatre, 35, 37
Sullivan, Charles, 67
Sullivan, John W., 62-63
Sundown, Jack, 135
Sunol, Antonio, 57
Sunsweet, 45
Swenson, Carl N., 82, 86
Taafe, Molly, 119
Tacoma Brewing Company, 139
Tamien Station, 85-86
Taylor, Mary, 4
Tennant, John, 14
The Alameda, 23, 35, 41, 55, 85-86, 115, 119
Thomas Flyer, 121-123
Thomas Motor Company, 121
Tisdale, Betty, 119
Towne Theater, 45
Trinity Episcopal Church, 95
Trinkler-Dohrmann, 75
Twain, Mark, 5
Twohy, John, 76
Twohy Building, 39, 45, 80, 91
U A Theatre, 37
Ulrich, R., 88
Unique Theater, 39
Unitarian, 16, 96, 118
Unitarian Church, 16, 96
University of San Francisco, 17
University of Santa Clara, 28, 86
University of The Pacific, 51-53, 55, 72, 134
University Park, 52, 54, 87
Vasquez, Tiburcio, 9, 30
Vendome Hotel, 100-101, 103, 114-115
Vicar of Wakefield, 40
Victory Theatre, 18, 36-37, 39, 96, 101
Victory Vitaphone, 36
Villa Montalvo, 19, 29, 70, 96
Village Amusement Park, 14
Villages, 67, 70
Vintage Towers, 80
Vivier, Armand, 123
Volstead Act, 62
Walker, Charlotte, 34

Walker, Rose, 137
Walley, Richard, 37
Walter, Carrie Stevens, 119
Walton, Richard, 32
Watkins, Laura, 119
Watson, Fred, 140
Watt, Keith, 46
Weeks, Charles P., 76
Weeks, H. H., 79, 99
Weeks, Harold, 82
Weeks, William, 26, 79, 82, 90, 101
Wehner, William, 67-70
Wehner Ranch, 68-69
Welch, Judge J. R., 22, 127
Wells Fargo, 44
Werner, Carl, 97
Western Flyer, 27
Whitton, A. K., 99
Wilbur, Brayton, 73
Wilde, Oscar, 47-48
William Wehner Estate, 67-70
Williams, Virgil, 110
Willow Glen, 41-42, 45-46, 86
Willow Glen Theater, 41, 45
Winchester Mystery House, 116
Wolf, F. D., 60
Wolfe and McKenzie, 58, 103
Wood, Donald, 106
Woodhills, 29-31
*WPA Guide*, 115
Wright, Frank Lloyd, 24
Wright, T. M., 62-63
Wykoff, Ralph, 97
Yaramie, Arthur, 42
YMCA Building, 44
York, Sidney, 119
Yosemite Valley, 110
YWCA, 75
Zeus, Carl, 119
Zust, 121, 123
Zuur, James, 41